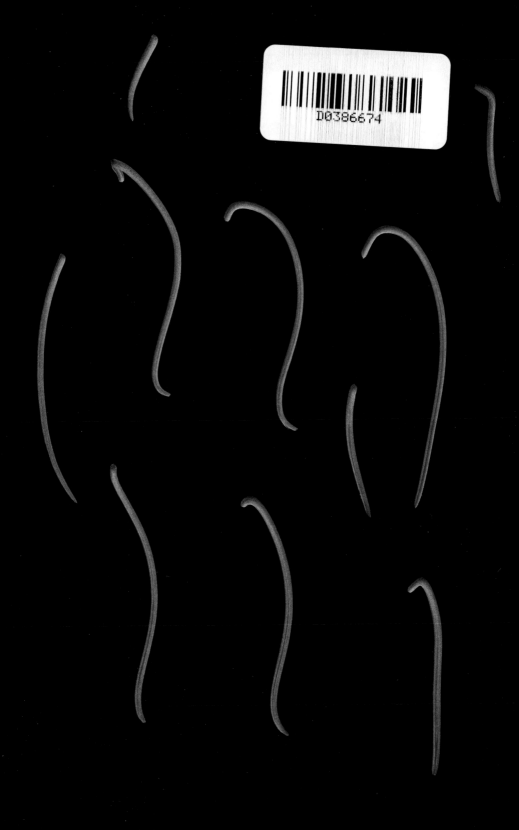

Acquainted
with Grief

Acquainted with Grief

Wang Mingdao's Stand
for the Persecuted Church in China

by
Thomas Alan Harvey

Brazos Press
A Division of Baker Book House Co
Grand Rapids, Michigan 49516

©2002 by Thomas Alan Harvey

Published by Brazos Press
a division of Baker Book House Company
P.O. Box 6287, Grand Rapids, MI 49516–6287

Printed in the United States of America

Library of Congress Cataloging-in-Publication Data

Harvey, Thomas Alan, 1956–
    Acquainted with grief : Wang Mingdao's stand for the persecuted church in
China / by Thomas Alan Harvey.
       p.   cm.
    Includes bibliographical references.
    ISBN 1-58743-039-8 (cloth)
    1. Wang, Mingdao, 1900–   2. China—Church history—20th century. I. Title.
BR1297.W3 H37 2002
275.1'082'092—dc21   2002011701

ISBN 1-58743-059-2 (intl. pbk.)

For current information about all releases from Brazos Press, visit our web site:
http://www.brazospress.com

Contents

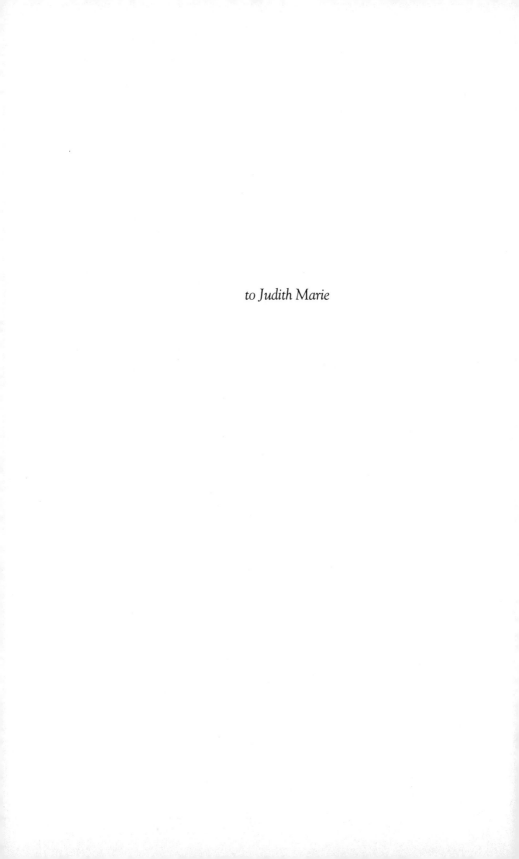

to Judith Marie

Introduction

"Understand two men, and you will understand Chinese Christianity," offered a wizened Beijing Christian to a Western reporter. "Which two?" queried the curious reporter, "Wang Mingdao and K. H. Ting!'" Contenders over the heart and soul of the Chinese church for four decades, Wang Mingdao and K. H. Ting first crossed polemical swords over which path Christianity should follow in China in the wake of the Communist revolution in 1949. To appease the government, K. H. Ting insisted that Christians were to be loyal to the state, to submit to ideological political remolding, and to worship in officially sanctioned churches. Wang Mingdao demurred, arguing that such union and ideological pressure gutted the church of its message and mission. Eventually Ting would be tapped to lead the state-sanctioned Protestant churches, whereas Wang would be publicly ostracized, arrested, and imprisoned for twenty years. Nonetheless, like a hungry ghost who refuses to depart the bailiwick of his agony, the specter of Wang Mingdao has haunted and divided Christianity in China ever since. Referred to as the "Dean of the House Churches," Wang Mingdao's resistance, persecution, suffering, and perseverance have come to symbolize the faith of tens of millions who now worship outside state-approved churches.

The Enduring Legacy of Wang Mingdao

By no means a complete biography of Wang Mingdao, still this work does seek to introduce Western readers to Wang Mingdao. Though well-recognized in Chinese Christian circles, he remains relatively unknown in the West. That is to our detriment, for this man's life is a remarkable tale that reflects the tumult, pathos, and remarkable perseverance of Christianity in China. Born in the midst of a revolutionary tempest and raised in poverty, Wang Mingdao rose to become one of the most controversial and consequential Christian leader the Chinese church has produced. Admired by many and reviled by others, Wang's message and ministry would play a critical part in the transformation of Chinese Protestantism from a fragile church of 100,000 souls threatened with annihilation at the turn of the twentieth century to become a faith that today claims anywhere from thirty to seventy million adherents.[2]

Wang Mingdao is best remembered for his dogged resistance to government-imposed Protestant union and coerced political indoctrination in China. This work explains and analyzes that resistance and the conflict it bred between Wang and the government. In particular, we will carefully examine Wang's biblical and theological defense of his stand as well as the arguments leveled against it.

Though the names Karl Barth and Dietrich Bonhoeffer come more readily to mind when thinking of Christians who resisted twentieth-century totalitarianism, Wang Mingdao's resistance may be more significant. The regime that Barth and Bonhoeffer defied is as distant as the old newsreels of Hitler's speeches, while the religious policy Wang resisted remains in place today, and the issues he raised continue to divide the church half a century later. Thus, this work provides a timely and thorough account as well as an analysis of the issues that divided Chinese Christians fifty years ago and their continued relevance to China today.

Theological debate over this conflict has not been restricted to China. From the conflict's first tentative volleys even to the present, sides were drawn both in and outside China for and against Wang's stand. These voices are crucial, for they expose the universal nature of the issues raised and their relevance far beyond the bamboo curtain that descended on China at mid-century. Of special note will be issues raised by Barth and Bonhoeffer that have been curiously forgotten or simply ignored when relocated from Nazi Germany to contemporary Asia. Such amnesia arises from hidden assumptions and theological reflexes of our modern age that many believed collapsed with the demise of the Third Reich. As I will show, the very ideology and theology that sanctioned Nazi suppression of Christian dissent remains alive and well in modern theological discourse and is utilized by those who defend Christianity's embrace of political ideology and justify the persecution of Christians who resist it.

We will also note how the progressive embrace of political ideology by Wang's antagonists steadily eroded the justification of the church that they championed. At the same time, the resistance to that ideology, decried as "otherworldly," "pietistic," and "escapist," not only thrust Wang into the national spotlight but has also remained relevant to the social, religious, and political fabric of China up to the present time. This inversion will be unpacked so that we may understand better why Wang's evangelical resistance to the "Social Gospel" paradoxically led to his national prominence and significance.

Finally, this work will examine Wang Mingdao's ongoing legacy. Though no individual can be credited with the massive underground Christian movement in China today, still, the appellation "Dean of the House Churches" suits Wang Mingdao well. His life, resistance, suffering, and perseverance bear the marks of the Chinese church. Even as his arrest and imprisonment marked the end of public defiance of the government, how much more did his reemergence from the Chinese gulag twenty years later embody a Christian faith that has not only survived but grown stronger in spite of its official banishment. Even now, a half-century after his conflict with the government and ten years after his death, the figure of Wang Mingdao haunts the government in house churches that share the legacy of his resistance. Indeed anyone who would plumb the depths of Christianity in China, must first come to understand Wang Mingdao.

ONE

What's in a Name?

The name given the violent upheaval that engulfed China in 1900–1901 often reveals more than the historical accounts of the events themselves. To the Boxers, or in Chinese the "Fists of Righteous Harmony," theirs was a glorious uprising to purge the empire of the social, moral, political, and spiritual filth forced upon China by foreign devils and their minions. Trained in the martial arts, the Boxers believed their fists could ward off European bullets through magical incantations and rigorous mental and spiritual training. Convinced of their powers, bands of Boxers fanned out across Northern China razing Christian missionary outposts and slaughtering all the missionaries and Chinese Christians unable to flee from their path.

For powerful Europeans, however, the "Boxer Rebellion" was a brazen assault upon their citizens, a violation of international treaty, and a grave threat to their pecuniary interests in China. Though initially overwhelmed by the fury of the Boxers that inundated much of Northern China, it would not be long before they assembled an international force to march on Beijing to crush the rebellion and to exact a crippling indemnity that would break the back of the Chinese empire for good as well as guarantee unfettered trade throughout the heart of China.

One can find both of these names in any good history of China. What one will not find is the name given these events by those who suffered most. Demonstrating their peculiar knack of finding glory in suffering and triumph in death, Chinese Christians honored the 231 missionaries, 4,000 Protestants, and 30,000 Catholic Christians who died in the uprising by referring to their slaughter as "The Great Martyrdom."[1]

It is fitting that Wang Mingdao, whose own life cannot be fully understood apart from this odd mix of suffering, glory, and hope, was born during the midst of this violent collision of worlds and worldviews. At the beginning of the violence, Wang's father, Dr. Wang Dehao, worked and lived at the Methodist Hospital in Beijing with his wife, Li Wenyi, now pregnant with their fifth child. Of their four previous children, only one, a daughter, still survived.

By May 1901, Beijing was inundated with Chinese and foreigners fleeing the violence and destruction of the Boxers. The refugees' horrifying tales of villages burned and Christians tortured and beheaded only deepened Wang Dehao and Li Wenyi's sense of impending doom. On June 13, imperial troops joined the Boxers and rampaged through the north of Beijing killing hundreds of Chinese Christians. Their mutilated corpses were left in the streets to sow panic among the foreigners who still remained. Every church and mission building in that part of the city was destroyed except the Methodist compound where Wang Dehao and his family lived. Only days before, a detachment of twenty U.S. Marines had been sent to protect the compound. They repulsed the initial assault by the Boxers after which an anxious lull in the fighting ensued. Fearing that the Boxers were gathering strength for a new assault, those in the compound decided to risk a break for the Foreign Legation to join the other expatriate forces that remained in Beijing. Somberly they made their perilous trek to the Foreign Legation.

> First in the ranks marched the twenty Marines followed by the missionary women and children. . . . Then came the one hundred and twenty-six school girls marching in simple quiet dignity as if they were on their way to a religious service or school exercise. Hundreds of Chinese women and little children followed by a large company of men and boys were next in order. The handful of missionary men, armed

with rifles or revolvers, closed the line of march. It was a brave, sad caravan proceeding on its way from danger to danger.[2]

Within the walls and sandbags of the Foreign Legation they joined 450 soldiers, 2,500 Chinese Christians, and 475 foreign civilians preparing for the impending siege. They did not have to wait long. The next day thousands of Boxers, joined by imperial troops, swarmed around the Legate. The Empress Dowager, monarch of the empire, declared war on all foreigners in China and ordered their extermination.

Wang Dehao scaled the wall of the compound and saw that the gathering masses of Boxers and soldiers had cut off any escape. One decisive assault would breach the defenses of the Legation, leaving all its occupants subject to the mobs. The horror of the grisly death that awaited a traitor to the empire gripped Wang Dehao. Thus, rather than wait for what appeared to be inevitable, he fashioned his own gibbet and hung himself in a quiet corner of the Legation. Summoned from her room, Li Wenyi looked on as they lowered her husband's dead body.

Remarkably, the decisive blow that Wang Dehao had feared never came. Confident in their mystical powers, the Boxers advanced upon the Legate alone or in small groups, dancing and crying out incantations to make their bodies impervious to the soldiers' bullets. Disordered and futile, these assaults were easily beaten back.

All the while, imperial forces kept up a noisy but ineffective bombardment. The commander of the imperial troops despised the Boxers and thus refused to deploy his heavy artillery to press their advantage. As a result, those in the Legate held out, and five weeks after Wang Dehao took his life, Li Wenyi gave birth to a son. The birth of a healthy son in such terrible circumstances led the boy's grandmother to name him Wang Tie or "Iron Wang."[3] It was a nickname that would stay with him the rest of his life.

Finally, after forty-five days, the siege was lifted as the Allied Expeditionary Force arrived in Beijing on August 14. The Boxers scattered, and the Empress Dowager evacuated with her officials to Xian. The foreign troops had no mercy on Beijing. They ransacked the city and razed the beautiful summer palace that had once graced the Western Hills. Those in the Legation slowly made their way back to their homes to see what could be salvaged. Li Wenyi had nowhere to go. With her husband dead, no place was reserved for her at the Methodist compound.

With forty taels of silver she received as her part of the indemnity paid by imperial throne for reparations, she purchased a house in Beijing on Gan-yu hutong (Precious Rain Street). To survive, she took on boarders. Wang Mingdao's earliest recollections recount the cast of characters with whom he grew up:

> food vendors, rickshaw pullers, barbers, cooks . . . and soldiers. The most intelligent could only recognize a few (Chinese) characters. As for morality, the situation can be imagined. Lying, cursing, gambling opium smoking, stealing, fighting, sexual immorality, and wicked practices of every kind. You name it—they did it.[4]

The tenants often refused to pay their rent and cursed Wang's mother when she demanded payment. Thus, relations were sour with the tenants and spilled over to affect the family, as Wang's mother grew increasingly bitter and depressed. Meanwhile, to help make ends meet, Wang fetched usable coal from rubbish bins for cooking and warmth. As for food, his mother despised cooking, so he and his sister normally had only one meal a day. This led both to malnutrition and frequent illnesses.

Small and thin, he remained "Iron Wang."[5] Chinese names were thought to bestow blessing, fortune, and virtue and even to affect one's fate, and "Iron" fit Wang well.

> Ever since I was small I have had a certain characteristic. No matter what issue arose unless I myself could see the rightness of a certain course of action, I would not blindly follow others. On the other hand, once I had seen the rightness of a certain course of action I would allow no obstacles to hinder me following it. I may be weak in body, but I am not weak in will.[6]

Wang's refusal to bend often led to brawls, most of which he lost. "I suffered, but I was able to open my mouth and bawl them out and curse them. I was often beaten, but never surrendered to brute force."

To get her son out of this coarse environment, Wang's mother saved enough money to have him board at the London Missionary Primary School in Beijing. Wang, however, remained street tough. On one occasion, some older boys decided to bully the younger students into shaving their own heads. Though Wang's terrified classmates shaved their heads, he refused. When the bullies threatened to shave only one side of his head while he slept if he didn't comply. Wang replied: "All right! But whoever dares to actually do it, I will take the scissors and stab out his eyes." Wang records that "no one made a move and my hair was preserved intact. It was I who claimed victory."[7]

At his enrollment Wang's mother gave him the name Wang Yongsheng, "Eternal Abundance." Once again, the name was fitting. He quickly ranked at the top of his class and was awarded a scholarship that covered board and lodging.

Like many of his generation, Wang was torn between veneration for ancient China and the desire for radical transformation of society. Given the political events that surrounded his growing up, this is not surprising. When Wang was eleven, the child emperor Pu Yi abdicated and turned power over to the Nationalist forces of Dr. Sun Yat-sen bringing four thousand years of dynastic rule to an end. As Wang and his classmates were led to the parade ground to raise the Nationalist Flag and to sing the national anthem "San Min Zhu Yi" ("The Three Principles of the People") they entered the ferment of a new age. Nonetheless, if Sun Yat-sen's three principles (nationalism, the rights of the people, and the prosperity of the people) represented a radical break from China's imperial past, what remained constant was the yearning for a powerful China that could stand its ground before the nations of the world.

This tension between the old and the new shaped Wang's character as well. "In me there are two instincts—one conservative and the other radical," he wrote. "If I considered a thing to be unalterable then not a shade of it could I allow to be altered. But if I considered a thing to be alterable then it must be altered thoroughly. Because of the presence of these two instincts many people were annoyed with me from my youth onwards."[8]

Having never known his father, Wang's first mentor was an older student who befriended him. Disciplined and devout, he encouraged Wang to order his life through prayer, Bible study, and starting a journal to keep track of his spiritual progress. Wang's fervent embrace of these provided the discipline he longed for but also the bitter pill of reproof: "Every time I erred in speech or conduct I would be grieved and reproached in heart, shedding tears over my sins which I confessed before God." This cycle of relentless pursuit of integrity and subsequent remorse in many ways was the engine that drove Wang onward to pursue personal perfection.

Wang's zeal for righteousness did not stop with himself. He was quick to point out flaws in others as well as in the institutions he found himself in. At the mission school, he grew indignant with the special treatment afforded to two wealthy boys who were allowed to run riot. Lewd and defiant, they harassed other students and even the teachers. When Wang went to the principal to complain, the principal weakly confessed that he could do nothing. Were their fathers to grow angry and withdraw their patronage, the school would go bankrupt. Better for the school to topple than to be corrupt, Wang retorted. "For believers in Christ to run a school in this way is to abandon Christian Principles."[9] When the two boys discovered Wang's attempt to have them expelled, they taunted him with the name "Dr. Morality" or simply "Pharisee." They would lie in wait to catch him falling short of his standards and then hurl further abuse at him. These taunts dug deep into Wang's soul and gave birth to a distinct disdain for the partiality shown the rich and powerful. In time, he would see it as the corruption devouring the soul of the church of which it was his God-given calling to expose and root out. Nonetheless, just as in primary school, this zeal for integrity in time would produce powerful enemies in the church.

The Roots of Independence: Politics, Pacifism, and Rebaptism

In his late teens and early twenties, Wang's inflexibility would profoundly shape his destiny. Keen to pursue a career in politics, Wang prepared for his university exams at a local college in Beijing. At the time, college campuses across Beijing were caught up in nationalist ardor. Frustration had been brewing ever since the Boxer uprising, as unequal treaties forced China to cede sovereignty over lucrative ports and provinces to Western nations, even as the country remained saddled with crippling indemnities in war reparations.

This chafed the soul of a people who in just a few decades had witnessed the dizzying collapse of their grand empire to a destitute vassal state carved up and apportioned to powerful foreign invaders. Particularly aggravating were Japanese claims, backed by corrupt Chinese officials, to Shandong province. In 1917 anger boiled over as anti-Japanese, pro-nationalist students formed unions to organize demonstrations, to distribute literature, and to foment anti-Japanese and anti-imperialist attitudes.

Student rallies to drum up patriotism became commonplace. Out of curiosity, Wang and his friends attended these rallies but studiously avoided joining the unions for fear it would jeopardize entrance into university. Nonetheless, at one rally they were enjoined from the rostrum to sign on with the union. Fear of being branded "traitors" convinced Wang's friends to join. Wang, however, stood up and refused. A shower of abuse fell on him. Denouncing him as a coward and a traitor, many threatened him with blows. His friends quickly deserted him for their own safety, and thus, angry and forsaken, Wang stormed out of the hall, his ears ringing with their abuse. He swore never to get involved in the "irrational passion of the nationalist movement," thus ending his pursuit of politics.[10]

New Directions

Wang's entrance exam scores were not high enough for him to enter Yenching University in Beijing, so he took a teaching position at the Presbyterian Primary School in Baoding, eighty miles south of Beijing. Although he earned only twelve dollars a month, he had enough to live on and was even able to send money home to his mother and sister.

At this time warlords and bandits roamed the Chinese country-side making a living through extortion, kidnappings, or threats of violence and mayhem against small villages and cities. In the winter of 1920, news of a warlord encamped near Baoding alarmed the city. The most tempting targets were the foreign missionaries, who were sure to fetch a handsome price if kidnapped.

Memory of the deaths only eighteen years earlier of nearly two hundred Chinese Christians and fifteen missionaries at the hands of the Boxers only heightened the anxiety in Baoding.[11] To discourage an attack, the Presbyterian school began training a militia made up of teachers and students. Wang became disturbed at the sight of daily marches and military drills in the school compound complete with guns provided by the Western Missionaries. Contending that such preparations violated what Jesus taught in the Gospels, Wang soon found himself in sharp disagreement with the missionary faculty. Wang argued that using violence against violence was not Christian and that "all who take the sword will perish by the sword" (Matt. 26:52). The only appropriate response of Christians was "to turn the other cheek." This upset the missionaries who argued sharply with him. Nonetheless, where foreign missionaries might have intimidated others, Wang refused to back down. Here at Baoding, Wang's disenchantment with the influence of foreign missionaries over the church in China would take root. In time Wang became convinced that it was high time for missionaries to return to their homes and for Chinese Christians to rise up and take their rightful place as leaders of the Chinese churches.[12]

A Passion to Reform the Church

"I felt strongly that the church needed a revolution and that the mission to bring about a revolution was entrusted to me."[13] These sentiments led Wang to change his name to Mingdao ("testify to the truth"). At Baoding, Wang's zeal for purity and truth was renewed. This zeal took an inward turn when a fellow teacher argued that Christians needed to be purified from all sin. Initially Wang scoffed: "How could any sin remain in a good Christian like me?" Nonetheless, his conscience was pricked, and soon Wang began to note character flaws in himself that he despised in others. "The more I prayed the more conscious I became of my unworthiness. I was unclean, vicious and hateful. . . . No matter how good a man is, only let him be illumined by the Spirit of God and he becomes conscious of his own utter depravity."[14] Wang's colleague pressed Wang to repent and dedicate his life fully to God for only then would he be truly purified. As a result, Wang's zeal for purity led to a commitment to fully serve God. In this commitment Wang experienced a spiritual transformation: "I was willing to obey him fully. I was ready to serve him faithfully all my life. From that day on my life was gradually but wonderfully changed."

Wang's colleague further argued that without proper baptism Wang's transformation would remain incomplete. He gave Wang some booklets on baptism, and Wang studied the relevant passages. These convinced him that his former baptism at the age of twelve in the Congregational Church had been invalid and that he required adult baptism and immersion. Meanwhile, however, the discovery by school officials that his colleague had been promoting rebaptism at a Presbyterian school resulted in his colleague's dismissal. The day of his departure, Wang escorted his friend to the train station. At their parting, Wang vowed, "I also am prepared to make sacrifices," and asked his friend to send someone to baptize him. A few weeks later a preacher named Zhu arrived in Baoding to meet with Wang and to prepare him for baptism.

The principal of the school, Thomas Biggin of England, had noted Wang's ability and zeal for ministry and had offered to raise money so Wang could travel to England to complete his education. When Biggin caught wind of Wang's desire to be rebaptized, he was deeply concerned and attempted to dissuade him. He warned Wang that rebaptism would mean disgrace and dismissal, ruining his last chance at a university education. Biggin urged Wang to take a few days to think it through. Two days later, Wang informed Biggin that if he were to delay baptism he would be "rebelling against God" and that "to obey is better than sacrifice" (1 Sam 15:22). Thus, Biggin informed him that he had no choice but to ask him to leave the following day.

Word of Wang's sacking soon spread among the students. Several visited his room that evening, and four students resolved to be rebaptized with Wang. At morning chapel, the principal announced Wang's departure and warned the students that if they followed his example they also would be expelled. This convinced a fifth student, Shi Tianmin, to join Wang and be rebaptized. Shi Tianmin's willingness to follow Wang would continue as they worked together in ministry over the next twenty-nine years.

Wang packed, left the school, and found rooms at a local inn. There Wang and the students met with the preacher Zhu from Beijing. It had snowed in Baoding for two days, so the next day they had to trudge through a fresh blanket of snow to find a suitable location for baptism. They went to the moat that surrounds the city but found it frozen over with thick ice. As they made their way along the moat, they finally came to a bridge where a small waterfall had created a pool suitable for baptism. After praying, Zhu entered the frigid water as Wang and the students took off their padded jackets and put on the thin baptismal garments. One by one they waded into the water and were baptized. As Wang was lifted out of the water, his long hair turned into thin icicles and his baptismal garments froze "hard and solid like thin boards."

When they returned to the inn, Zhu directed Wang and the students to "seek the Holy Spirit," exhorting them for two days to speak in tongues as a sign of the Holy Spirit. The five students spoke in tongues, but Wang, in his words, only "produced some incomprehensible sounds." Although Zhu announced that Wang had indeed spoken in tongues, Wang felt no different. On later reflection, Wang recorded that his experience of the fullness of the Spirit had taken place with his earlier repentance and commitment to serve God.

Crisis and Calling

Wang returned to Beijing with no job and no prospects. His mother was furious, and his elder sister railed against his selfishness and stubbornness. With the loss of his income, they would now have to struggle just to eat.[15] This reaction was not unexpected, but it hurt Wang deeply just the same. In Chinese culture, a virtuous son cares for his mother and siblings, yet Wang's mother and sister were already in poor health due to malnutrition. With no excuse to offer, Wang consigned himself to housework under the reproachful eyes of his mother and sister. The neighbors and tenants ridiculed him and his aunt claimed that he was mentally unstable and would amount to nothing.

Long hours with nothing to do soon led to despair. Wang looked for work but found none. To occupy himself, he fashioned the garden shed at the side of the house into a small study. Here, in what he would later describe as "God's Bible School," his failure, shame, and despair enlightened his reading of the Bible. As Wang explained, "Some of God's promises are written as it were in invisible ink. It is only when they are placed in the flame of suffering they become manifest."[16] During what he described as his "time in the wilderness," Wang concluded that a university degree was merely pursuit of "empty glory and fame." What he needed instead was to "be trained and taught by God."

In time Wang received an invitation from his cousin to spend two months at the cousin's small village in the mountains. Wang accepted, eager to get away from the tense and depressing situation at home. The village sat at the foot of Crouching Tiger Mountain. Each morning Wang would ascend the mountain to spend the day in study, prayer, and singing. His spirit refreshed, he soon began to read whole books of Scripture in one sitting. In two months he read through the entire Bible six times and, as he recorded later, "made considerable strides in my understanding of the truth."

As his mountain retreat neared its end, Wang received a letter from an old friend who had heard a rumor that Wang was "mentally ill." To convince his friend otherwise, Wang traveled to Tianjin to allow his friend to judge his mental fitness for himself. Impressed with Wang, the friend invited him to his church to preach. Wang's preaching was well received, and he was invited to return soon.

Wang recalled, "I went back to Beijing greatly comforted and encouraged. I was comforted because a respected friend had seen what the grace of God had done for me. I was encouraged because when I preached I was deeply conscious of the presence of God and enabled to speak with power and authority."[17] Wang's reputation as a gifted preacher soon spread, and by the end of the summer, invitations to preach began to pour in. With each engagement, Wang's reputation grew, and within the year Wang was receiving invitations to preach from across the country.

Over the next ten years Wang Mingdao would move from obscurity to prominence as one of the most influential preachers in China. Wherever he went large audiences flocked to hear him preach: "spellbound on his every word."[18] In 1927 he spent six months touring churches in southeastern China. In 1932 he went on six evangelistic tours across China. By 1948 he had preached in twenty-four of China's twenty-eight provinces.

Wang Mingdao's attack on corruption, his call to integrity and purity, and his independence struck a chord with his audiences and allowed him to cut away at the gangrenous corruption that had hobbled the church for nearly two decades. The first ten years of the twentieth century had witnessed a surge in conversions to Christianity, but by the 1920s that early growth had produced problems. Clergy and lay leadership lacked depth. Many had converted merely for material advantage, and many in pastoral ministry were more interested in the crumbs that fell from the foreign missionary's table than with the gospel itself. As a result, the Chinese populace held Christians in general and clergy in particular in low regard. They called them "rice Christians"— lackeys who would do anything to please their foreign masters.

With corruption rife and standards low, Wang's indictment of the church's lack of discipline and spiritual poverty struck a nerve. Weary of the rot and hungry for revival, Christians and non-Christians alike responded to his call for repentance, conversion, piety, and discipline. Wang attacked toady church leaders, confronted modernist and liberal pretense, and challenged previously unchallenged Western missionaries. At one conference he listed the biblical and theological errors of a previous speaker at the conference who had belittled biblical authority. This criticism, rather than hurting his reputation, resonated with Christians suspicious of prominent leaders but without the confidence to articulate their concerns.

Wang's success was not limited to the ministerial sphere but extended to his personal life. Wang's tours led to several preaching engagements in Nanjing, the ancient southern capital of China, where he stayed with a Pastor Liu and his family. Their home, unlike Wang's in Beijing, was a place of warmth, laughter, and harmony. In some ways, he regarded Pastor Liu as the father he had never known. When he first visited he took little notice of their daughter Jingwen, but in time he came to notice her and his attraction grew. Her family, her disposition, and her faith made her a good match for Wang. Thus, in the style of that time, Wang sent a Christian "sister" to Pastor and Mrs. Liu to make a proposal of marriage. Against the tradition of that time, they left it up to Jingwen. She accepted, saying simply, "What my heavenly Father sees is good, I see as good."[19]

The match, however, could not be finalized until Wang's mother approved. His mother referred to lodgers from the south as "southern barbarians" and generally looked down on anyone not from Beijing. Expecting the worse, Wang informed his mother of his proposal. He took it as a minor miracle and a confirmation of God's approval when his mother offered no objection. Thus, on November 26, 1926, Wang Mingdao and Liu Jingwen were married. They would have one son, Tianduo.

It was not an easy life. They moved in with Wang's mother and sister. As an outsider, Jingwen was either coldly ignored or scolded whenever she erred in any task. Filial piety demanded that Wang not intervene but rather honor his mother and sister's place to rule the home. Nonetheless, Jingwen rarely complained and put up with much grief and ill treatment. In 1931, Jingwen contracted tuberculosis. The doctor ordered her to move to a sanitarium to heal, but Wang's mother and sister refused to permit her to leave, claiming that the doctor's diagnosis was in error. As Jingwen's condition worsened, Wang feared for her life. Wang begged his mother to relent and finally was granted permission to allow Jingwen to go to the sanitarium, where she slowly regained her health.

Wang Mingdao and Liu Jingwen were of different demeanors, which led to periodic friction between them. Since each had a strong personality and refused to give in easily, they often quarreled over trivial matters. At first this irritated Wang, who had his way with most people outside his home. Over time, however, he came to see that friction as the hand of God to "rub off our corners so that we might both become smooth stones." At the age of fifty, Wang summed up his marriage as follows:

> It is nearly 22 years since my wife and I were married. Although we once passed through a long period of friction we still maintained our trust in each other. We did not tell each other lies, nor did we harbor suspicions about each other. We did not deceive each other. We were loyal in our friendship and sincere in our relationship.[20]

The suffering and toil of those years are not recorded by Liu Jingwen, but as hard as they were they could not compare to what they would experience in the difficult years ahead.

Evangelical Revival in China and the Independent Chinese Churches

Wang's meteoric rise in prominence was not a singular phenomenon. This period also saw the rise of Watchman Nee, John Sung, David Yang, and Marcus Cheng—all of whom along with Wang stressed repentance, conversion, holiness, doctrine, and discipleship. They were the vanguard of a revival that swept through the Chinese churches of the late 1920s and early 1930s. Evangelical and antiliberal, they decried the leadership of modernists and liberals in the churches. To the chagrin of some church leaders, seminary lecturers, and liberal Protestant missionaries, they argued that those who cast doubt on Scripture, the resurrection, and Christ's future return were not simply in error but anti-Christian and poisoning the church in China by spreading unbelief.

This ferment and controversy ignited the evangelical wing of the Chinese Christian churches and they grew significantly. Several of these leaders, including Wang Mingdao, established independent Chinese churches with no denominational ties or foreign missionary influence. Whereas independent and indigenous churches had been virtually nonexistent in 1930, by 1948 independent indigenous churches represented a quarter of all Protestants in China. This institutional independence only deepened the doctrinal chasm between conservatives and liberals in China. Not only were the independent churches more conservative and evangelical than their denominational cousins, but their institutional separation led the independent churches to see no need for integration with the denominational churches in any areas of faith and practice. Further, the growth of independent churches widened the chasm between conservatives and liberals within the mainline denominational churches themselves. Although his own church was independent, Wang maintained friendships and what he regarded as "spiritual relationships" with pastors and churches within the mainline denominations. After 1949, these links would make it difficult for the then Communist government to move against Wang Mingdao for fear of alienating other churchmen who knew and respected him. Moreover, this split between conservative and liberal would directly impact the great divide in the church that lay just over the horizon with the gathering storm of the Communist Revolution. Liberal and conservative camps within Christianity would respond quite differently to that storm, whose fury would indelibly change China and the Chinese church.

TWO

A Church Divided

Modernism, Fundamentalism,
and the Anti-Christian Movement

As the soul of a nation crying out for freedom and democracy, the thousands of students who filled Beijing's Tiananmen Square on May 4, 1919, ushered the modern age into China. The May Fourth Movement began with the news that Chinese officials had conceded former German-held Chinese territory and ports to Japan. Failure to regain Chinese sovereignty over her own territory because of corrupt officials and Japan's imperial designs let loose a torrent of rage against those who had sold out China. Anger gave way to violence as rampaging students seized and beat a pro-Japanese official and burned to the ground a Cabinet Minister's house. After the initial conflagration died down, nationalist passions continued to burn within China's scholars and students. They wanted to transform China by casting off the superstition and feudalism that left her weak and at the mercy of more powerful nations. This intellectual ferment gave rise to a radical intellectual, social, and economic revolution in China that sought to trump superstition with science, overcome feudalism with modern nationalism and cast off China's regressive past for a new progressive social order.

It wasn't long before the scholars leading this movement turned their focus upon the role of religion in Chinese society. Leading intellectuals trained in European and American universities argued that religion in general and Christianity in particular were based on obsolete superstitions. As a "reactionary force in modern society," religion only perpetuated the stifling status quo.[1] Though they recognized that Christians had come to China with good intent, they had now become a negative force in society as they reinforced patterns and attitudes of docile submission to foreign imperialism. This criticism gathered institutional momentum in 1922 when a group of scholars and students established an "Anti-Christian Movement" to mitigate the negative influence of Christianity. They argued that the continued presence and privileges granted Christian missionaries in China should be ended and the universities, colleges, schools, and hospitals built and run by missionary agencies should be turned over to the Chinese to manage and run. They demanded that Christian colleges, schools, orphanages, and hospitals be nationalized and made secular institutions. Some went so far as to argue that to be Christian was tantamount to being anti-Chinese.

Two paths emerged amongst Chinese Christians to address anti-Christian sentiments. One path was modernist and defended Christianity as a rational, practical, and relevant faith well suited to address the problems facing the Chinese people. The other path was evangelical and sought to establish an indigenous church no longer dependent upon foreign missionaries and their corrupting influence. These two paths were bound to cross given that their intellectual, social, and theological perspectives were sharply at odds. Each saw the other as a hindrance to the establishment of a vital and relevant Christian faith in China.

The Modernist Defense of Christianity in China

In 1922, Chinese Christian intellectuals found themselves in a difficult position. As scholars, students, and loyal Chinese, they shared the nationalist aspirations of the May Fourth Movement and agreed that the time of foreign domination of Christian schools, hospitals, and denominational churches had come to an end. Nonetheless, as Christians they strenuously rejected the notion that their faith was anti-Chinese. Rather than abandon their faith, they chose to defend it.[2]

In 1922 a handful of Chinese Christian intellectuals were associated with the YMCA. Mostly teachers at Christian colleges and universities, some had attained master's and doctoral degrees from leading universities in America and Britain. Educated during the heyday of Social Gospel, they readily embraced its practical concern for science, progress, and social justice. Here was a gospel that was relevant to the social and political problems that bedeviled their homeland. The problem was not with Christianity properly understood, but with overemphasis on personal piety that had kept Christians from addressing social and political reform. When Christian scholars returned to China from America and Europe, they brought back what they believed was a modern, progressive, and rational faith ready to address the issues that confronted the nation.

In response to the Anti-Christian Movement, members of the YMCA formed the Peking Apologetic Group to rebut charges that Christianity was regressive, reactionary, and anti-Chinese. Their central tenet was that "Christianity is the greatest need in connection with the regeneration of the Chinese society and that the spreading of Christianity is our greatest obligation."[3] In line with the Social Gospel, "regeneration" now became central to Chinese society as a whole and not merely an aspect of personal conversion. In this regard, Christianity proved its worth. If science could overwhelm ignorance and superstition and democracy could overcome feudal tyranny, then Christianity could provide the spiritual regeneration necessary to overcome the lethargy and fatalism that bedeviled China. What was needed was a faith to motivate the people to embrace national reconstruction.

Among the members of this group, two scholars in particular stood out from the rest: T. C. Chao and Y. T. Wu. Both were closely associated with the YMCA in Beijing, both had done extensive graduate study in theology in the United States, and both sought to establish the truths of the Social Gospel in China. Chao, a graduate of Vanderbilt

University with bachelor of divinity and master of arts degrees, taught sociology of religion at Suzhou University and later served as dean of Yenching University. In 1948 he was elected one of six vice-presidents of the World Council of Churches in Amsterdam. Y. T. Wu, his contemporary, studied at Union Theological Seminary in New York, received his masters from Columbia University, and later returned to Union to study under Reinhold Niebuhr. Wu was chief editor of the YMCA's Association Press and active in the World Student Christian Federation.

T. C. Chao sought to respond to those who attacked Christianity as politically useless and socially enervating. Chao argued that strong social foundations require strong spiritual foundations. Indeed, what China lacked was the "moral excellence" required for individual and social transformation. "Moral excellence" was something Christianity could produce in China, for Jesus Christ was the ultimate model of "moral excellence." Chao believed that history was replete with many saviors that modeled ethical and intellectual "excellence," including Plato and Socrates of the West as well as Confucius and Buddha in the East. What set Jesus apart was his unsurpassed moral character and redemptive personality. This made Christ the way and the truth of "moral excellence" for a nation combating endemic corruption, vice, and moral ineptitude.[4]

> The erasure of sin from the heart of every individual means nothing short of social reconstruction. Indeed it means social reconstruction! . . . The heart of the problem of reconstruction, beyond any doubt, is the creation of a new spirit in men. This only Christianity can do.[5]

Coined as "Christian Reformism," Chao's defense of Christianity rested on the belief that, with Jesus as the exemplar, Christian influence and engagement could serve the nation by providing the moral foundation necessary to build a just and prosperous society.

For Y. T. Wu, Christianity was a "rational faith to supply the driving power of doing good."[6] Thus, for Wu, the true "principles of Christianity" were revealed in social progress.[7] In fact, Wu argued that Christianity was simply another name for the spirit of truth that underlies all phenomena. That is, "There is only one common truth which permeates the universe. This truth is that which unites and controls the phenomena of the universe so that it is a 'universe' and not a 'multiverse.' "[8] This principle had been discovered in Christianity in what Wu referred to as "the way of love." Although all religions expressed this "way" in some manner, only Jesus revealed "the way of love" that leads to social redemption.

As the means of social transformation, Wu was convinced that Jesus' "way of love" was relevant to China. Though the vanguard of this "way" were the social, scientific, political, and economic revolutions shaping the twentieth century, Wu was convinced that Christianity provided crucial insight into the spiritual nature of these materialist revolutions. Wu argued that pietistic Christianity had separated the Spirit from the material and become shackled by meaningless ritual, irrelevant preaching, and ignorant fundamentalism. This led to it being threatened by real progress and thus had made the church largely a reactionary force in history opposed to progress. Nonetheless, Wu believed that with Christian faith's unique perception of social redemption in hand, it could rise up and provide the spiritual framework necessary to fully grasp and guide the progressive forces of history arising in China.

This could only occur, however, if Christians were willing to recognize that the Spirit of God was leading the materialist revolutions of the day to address the real needs of the people. Wu argued that meeting these needs was in fact the true realization of the Kingdom of God on earth. For Wu, the "Kingdom" was the ideal state where humankind would be liberated from persecution, oppression, injustice, and where physical, emotional, and material needs were met. Thus the Kingdom was relevant to China, for the nation's greatest needs were economic, social, and material. As Wu argued, for the kingdom to be realized in China, "new roads have to be built, mines opened, factories operated, machines installed in all sorts of industrial enterprises."[9]

Not surprisingly, Wu's sympathies turned toward Marxism and the cause of the Chinese Communist party in the 1940s. In Marxism and Communism, Wu saw a force that could actually transform China.

Though disappointed with the continued influence and ultimate failure of Christian fundamentalism and pietism in China, Wu looked
to the forces of Communist materialism to usher in the divine transformation of society.[10] After the outbreak of the Sino-Japanese war
in 1937, Wu openly supported the Chinese Communist Party. In 1943
he met Party Secretary Zhou Enlai, and in 1948 he wrote "The Present Day Tragedy of Christianity," in which he argued that God's will
was being revealed in the inexorable tide of revolution sweeping across
China.

In Wu's view, the time had come for the church to abandon its
reactionary attitude toward the revolution. Rather than fight the
tide of progress, the church should join with the undeniable Spirit
of God at work in the revolution. To stand in its way was foolish,
and those who did would be swept away by the progressive force of
history.[11] Wu's article created such a storm that he was forced to
resign as editor of *Tian Feng*, the most influential Christian academic
journal in China, only to take up his position a few months later
when the Communists came to power. When, in 1949, the new premier Zhou Enlai looked for someone to represent the concerns of
the new government to the Christian churches, he turned to Y. T.
Wu. Together they would plan the future of Christianity in the new
Republic of China.

Uneasy with a divine Jesus and personal salvation, Chao and Wu
sought to salvage Christianity by emphasizing aspects of Jesus and
Christian faith that enhanced the cause of national liberation. For
Chao, the focus was on the Jesus who modeled the moral excellence
necessary for national salvation. For Wu, Jesus was the great revolutionary whose way of love would topple the corrupt social and political structures that oppress humankind. Although they disagreed in
the details, both believed that, for Christianity to survive, it would
have to ride with the tide of social and political liberation crashing
upon China. Thus Wu wrote:

> Christianity must learn that the present period is one of liberation for
> the people, the collapse of the old system, a time when the old dead
> Christianity must doff its shroud and come forth arrayed in new gar-
> ments. . . . It is no longer the sole distributor or the panacea for the

pains of the world. . . . God has taken the key to the salvation of mankind from its hand and given it to another.[12]

Anti-Christian, Anti-Western Attitudes, and the Evangelical Revival

The formal Anti-Christian Movement may have been confined to colleges and government halls in Beijing and Shanghai, but anti-Christian, antimissionary feelings were strong throughout China. Whereas T. C. Chao and Y. T. Wu used the Social Gospel to parry the blows aimed at their faith by unbelieving scholars, Wang Mingdao tapped into anti-Western and antimissionary sentiments to call for independence and revival.

Wang was appreciative of Western missionaries who had brought the gospel to China at great sacrifice. That era, however, had passed and the foreign missionaries that remained had now become a liability to Christianity in China. Even though Western missionary agencies spoke of indigenous leadership, they continued to hold the purse strings that paid the salaries and built the churches in China. The new vision of the Social Gospel had actually made matters worse, as concern for evangelism gave way to social reconstruction. This meant the primary work and money of the church was directed to building and staffing hospitals, schools, orphanages, universities, and medical colleges. In turn, this required money, bureaucracy, and accountability, and where money was involved it remained under the control of a Western administrator. In the end, all this fostered dependency and parasitism among Chinese pastors and church leaders.

This dependency grated on Chinese sensibilities. It was a constant reminder that their country was weak, poor, dependent, over-run by foreigners, and entirely lacking in self-respect. Worse, Western money and power attracted and rewarded parasites who fawned after Western missionaries in hope of securing steady employment. Thus, when Wang Mingdao and other evangelists spoke against corruption and preached independence, they scratched their listeners' antiforeign itch.

Nevertheless, Chinese angst went far deeper than antiforeign ardor. Living in a society on the brink of upheaval, people grew anxious with the growing anarchy, the talk of revolution, and the presence of the bellicose Japanese. In a disordered world, the practical insight, self-discipline, and promise of divine succor offered by evangelists such as Wang Mingdao provided courage and hope in an increasingly desperate situation. Wang's audiences were not intellectuals, but common people, and his message was tailored to meet their needs. To those outside the church, he preached repentance, conversion, and salvation. He exhorted them to turn away from idols and superstition and to put their faith in Christ and to join the church. To those in the church he preached separation from corruption and a life of simplicity, purity, faith, and discipline. To the clergy, Wang preached repentance and integrity exhorting them to separate themselves from modernist "false prophets," whom he denounced from the pulpit and attacked with the pen.[13]

Repentance and Conversion

The central pillar of Wang's message was repentance and conversion.

Without doubt those who genuinely believe in the Lord Jesus will first have repented before God. . . . It is necessary first to repent before you can speak in terms of believing in the Lord Jesus. . . . We need first to make people aware of their sin and of the painful consequences of sin.[14]

Having grown up in a rogue's gallery, Wang's message was good news for those wishing to escape the snare of vice. The rabid pursuit of wealth, power, influence, and pleasure ended only in bondage. The only way to be set free was through faith in Christ whereby the "love of sinning gives way to love of holiness and virtue."[15] All that bedeviled the world, whether sickness, evil, bloodshed, violence, or disease, found its root in "evil desire" and the personal and social disorder that flowed from it. Only through grace, faith, and discipline could order and purity be restored.

Through the preaching of the saving grace of God countless numbers have been saved. They have turned to God in repentance and faith and their lives have been wonderfully transformed. Even the hardhearted and the loveless have confessed their sins before God. Those who once regarded themselves as righteous have humbled themselves before God and have bowed before him in contrition.

Even as figures such as Y. T. Wu disdained emphasis on repentance and conversion as irrelevant self-centered piety, Wang argued repentance and conversion was the first step to real transformation.

People who were once fierce and violent have become like sheep. People who once sought their own interests now seek the interests of others. People who were once discouraged are now aflame with zeal. Those who were once broken-hearted and those who once wept are now greatly comforted. The protagonists of the social gospel criticize these people and condemn their activities as emotional and they charge these people with being superstitious and deceived. The fact is, not only does the preaching of the social gospel fail to get better results than this, they even fail to match up to them.[16]

Though the above might appear similar to T. C. Chao's view that only reformed people could reform society. What in fact Wang argued was that through repentance and conversion an alternative to the vice and corruption that poisons all life was available in the church.

Purification of the Chinese Church

In short, conversion meant movement from confusion to clarity, disorder to order through faith in Jesus Christ and the application of sound doctrine to the practical matters of life. This fusion of religious faith, doctrine, and the practical discipline of a holy life struck home with his audiences. After thirty years of social and political upheaval, corruption, and banditry, Wang's message resonated with the felt need in China to reestablish ethical society.

The term for "ethics" in Chinese is *Daode*. *Dao* literally means "the path or way," but it also refers to truth or doctrine. Accordingly, doctrine and life are inextricably intertwined and when ordered properly they produce excellence (*de*). Thus, the *Daode* refers to the way, the life, and the truth of excellence. In turn Christ is the ultimate teacher and example of the *Daode*. As Wang explained:

> By his [Christ's] own holy and blameless life He did two things. On the one hand He exposed the depravity of the people. On the other hand through His teaching and preaching, and through all that he did—culminating in His glorious resurrection—He showed men *the path that they should follow and the duties that they should perform* (emphasis added).

Accordingly, the church should exemplify the "life of Christ" and thus embody and witness the *Daode* of Christ. According to Wang,

> He [Christ] raised up certain people to whom He said, "You are the light of the world!" Who are these people? Can it be other than those of us who are His disciples? What a marvelous mandate! What a noble calling! Since we are to be "the light of the world" in the same way that He was "the light of the world," then our words and deeds, like those of the Lord, ought always to be throwing light on the path of the people in darkness.[17]

Once again we see the social ramifications of Wang's message. Life was a matter of paths. Those outside Christ walked in darkness, but those who followed the path (*Dao*) of Christ offered an alternative and example of how life should be lived. Again resonating with China's ancient ethical tradition, Wang offers the life of Christ, the true sage, as a way (*dao*) now modeled, ordered, and embodied through the way (*dao*) of his followers.

> When an artist paints a picture or does a carving, he places an actual object in front of him, and with this before him he paints his picture or does his carving. We call that object a model. Every Christian ought to be a model, a pattern. Thus if people are ignorant as to how they should order their life, all they need to do is to watch a Christian and then they should know. But the fundamental question is this, how many Christians today are in a position to serve as patterns for others? How many are worthy to be patterns?[18]

Wang's emphasis on the *Daode* of Christ complicates the common dismissal of Wang's message as "otherworldly," a mere escape from the harsh reality of everyday life.[19] Wang's message was extremely practical. He desired to establish a peculiar people whose faith and discipline had practical social consequences. Thus he wrote:

> There are indeed a few Christians in the world who are engaged in spreading the light, but unfortunately their efforts are limited to words. They can preach quite acceptably; they can describe the beauties of the Lord; and they can indicate the path that men should follow. But before long their own shadow obscures this good teaching. For there is a considerable difference between what they say and what they do.[20]

For Wang Mingdao, the great need in the world was for God's way to be manifest in the world through the church. Because of this, Wang strove not so much to create huge followings but to ensure that those who followed Christ offered a model for people to follow.[21]

Thus Wang railed against corruption in the churches of China. Corrupt churches had no gospel to offer; instead, like ancient Israel their paths had become disordered by the ways of the fallen world and thus led to darkness and death. In Wang's words,

> God had commanded those who belong to Him to come out from unbelievers and to be separate from them. Yet the Church of the present-day persists in following worldly ways and in going hand in hand with those who are God's enemies. Just as Israel of old disobeyed God's commands and copied the evil ways of Canaan, so does the Church of today ignore God's teaching and copy the evil customs of the world.[22]

Thus, purifying the church was essential and purification demanded exposing the corrupt practices of Christians and Christian leaders. Many felt the lash of Wang's biting criticism—particularly church leaders who benefited from Western missionary coffers. But Wang's criticism was not limited to the church leaders; he also chastised foreign missionaries who supported "double faced small men" who toadied up to the foreigner only for financial security and prestige.[23]

Though Wang's drive for purity eventually led to the establishment of a church independent of denominational and mission ties, he still maintained friendships with and continued to minister in churches across denominational lines. This helped to build strong bonds with others who shared his concern over corruption and the need for purity. These compatriots also shared Wang's antipathy toward highly placed liberals and modernists in the denominational hierarchy whose teaching, they believed, had been corrupted by Western liberal Protestantism.

Challenging the Preachers of "Another Gospel"

Whereas repentance, grace, and discipline addressed dependency and corruption in the church, the far deadlier toxin, in Wang's estimation, was the message of Christian liberals and modernists. He viewed their attempt to fuse the gospel with the popular cause of national salvation as heresy. His fierce conflict with the religious authorities in the 1950s was actually the culmination of a thirty-year crusade to warn the church of the dangers of modernists in their midst.

The modernist-fundamentalist debate first arrived on China's shores between the World Wars as newly trained missionaries sought to replace what they regarded as an antiquated concern to save lost pagan souls with a relevant Social Gospel that addressed the immediate physical and social needs of the people. This led to intense activity to establish schools, hospitals, and charitable institutions and to present Christianity as a progressive and scientific faith attuned to the social and political realities of China. This, it was argued, could only occur if the superstitious chafe that hid the relevant truth of the Bible were removed. Fractious debates arose between modernist and fundamentalist missionaries over the nature of faith, revelation, and Christian missions. These disputes quickly spilled over into churches, denominations, and parachurch organizations. Thus, the modernist-fundamentalist debate now found itself on Chinese soil with Chinese proxies who sought to make sense of this debate in light of the struggles facing Chinese Christians and the wider society.

As far as Wang Mingdao was concerned, modernists, whether Chinese or Western, preached "another gospel" that had exchanged the kingdom of God for a lesser kingdom of social improvement. T. C. Chao's all-too-human Jesus made Christ's atonement absurd and his resurrection mere myth. Y. T. Wu had sold out sanctification for dubious social and political progress. For Wang Mingdao, Chao and Wu had dumped the gospel and now offered the faithful mere placebos that could never get at the root of human misery and social disorder. He explained:

> Obviously we . . . recognize the need to eliminate killing and violence and robberies and diseases and pain—all of which characterize life in society today. But we ought also to understand that all these calamities are ultimately the result of sin. So long as you do not solve the question of sin you cannot even begin to talk about anything else.[24]

The danger of modernists such as Wu and Chao was that their myopic focus on personal and social reconstruction had blinded them to humankind's most critical need: the need to be reconciled with God. Wang asked:

> What is the greatest need of mankind? Is it extravagant clothes? Is it lavish food? Is it a congenial occupation? Is it adequate medical provision? Is it upright politics? Is it a comprehensive system of law? Is it a higher level of society? Is it harmony among the nations? Is it the reform of our habits? Is it the establishment of virtue? All these are the needs of mankind. But the greatest need of all is not among them. Mankind's greatest need is to come to God for forgiveness of sin in order to have eternal life. Whether people acknowledge it or not, their greatest need is to be brought into touch with God. For God is the source of all happiness. But they have been cut off from God by sin and they themselves are unable to bridge the gap. What else can people do but endure pain and await the onset of death?[25]

Those who championed the Social Gospel charged that evangelists such as Wang Mingdao were irrelevant and escapist; they offered no word to the masses yearning for justice and human liberation. What good was a gospel that only offered an illusory promise of eternal life before an ever-receding day of judgment? These fundamentalists, in the modernists' estimation, offered nothing to deal with real issues facing the people of China.

Beneath the harsh rhetoric, the true divide between Chinese modernists and fundamentalists lay not in the goal of social improvement but in the means for achieving it. According to the modernists, social reconstruction required the reformation of political institutions or individuals so that they might serve and support the common aspirations and projects of the entire nation. In Wang Mingdao's view, social reconstruction would come through the church. The church's purpose, however, was not to serve and support the flawed social and political vision of a corrupt society but to offer a clear alternative based on the great ends of the church. For Wang, the disorder of the fallen world should never set the agenda for the church. In contrast, modernists looked to the secular to establish the arena, the rules, and the goals of society in which God was at work to bring about the kingdom of God. The only question in their minds was whether the church would keep in step or be swept aside as a useless hindrance to the progress of God.

From 1924 up to his arrest in 1955 by the Communist government, Wang would find his chief opponents in those who saw the kingdom of God realized in the secular transformation of society. Ever the combatant, he lashed out at their message. These attacks by Wang were by no means debates, and it would appear that for the most part these two camps were content to preach to the converted within their own circles. Nonetheless, in a sermon in 1947, Wang foreshadowed the coming storm that would overwhelm him in the revolution that would forever change China.

> I cannot do other than to oppose those who preach merely the social gospel. They do not attack me first, but they will certainly mount a counter-attack. I recognize that this is inevitable, but I do not shrink from the encounter nor do I seek to evade it. For the sake of the commission that God has entrusted to me, for the protection of the Church, for the good of mankind, and for the glory of God—for all these reasons I must oppose the social gospel and warn those who preach it.[26]

Wang's assault was not limited to the pulpit. By the mid-1920s, Wang had begun to write and publish booklets addressing critical issues of doctrine and practice in the Chinese church. In 1927 he launched a journal entitled *Spiritual Food Quarterly (Lingshi Jikan)*[27] on a shoestring budget. It featured his commentary on Scripture as well as his views on issues facing Christians in China. At first Wang sent the journal just to a few friends and churches, but the circulation of *Spiritual Food Quarterly* grew steadily until it was distributed to churches in every province in China. Wang's notoriety and influence grew as a result. Wang kept this periodical in print all the way up to his arrest in 1955.

Up to the 1930s, arguments between modernists and fundamentalists were mostly confined to Western missionaries in urban centers, but journals such as *Spiritual Food Quarterly* widened the debate to include Chinese churches throughout the nation. In this manner, the influence of Wang Mingdao and the fault lines of the modernist-fundamentalist divide could not be cordoned off to within the urban centers, but had extended outward to affect all of the churches in China. Further, Wang's writings also found a readership outside of China amongst the Chinese diaspora throughout Asia. His autobiography *Wu Shi Nian Lai (After Fifty Years)* was printed in 1950 and was well received in Hong Kong and Taiwan.[28] Thus, by 1949, Wang's reputation throughout the churches in China as well as his international following made him a difficult figure to silence or remove without the Christian world taking notice.

Founding an Indigenous Church

In 1924, Wang began to hold two meetings a week at his home in Beijing where Wang would preach to the dozen or more friends and interested parties that would gather. As attendance grew, the group could no longer fit into Wang's house. Thus they moved the meetings to a larger home that could accommodate seventy people and increased the number of services to four per week. In 1933 a hall was rented that could seat two hundred persons with room for another one hundred in the courtyard. In the winter when the temperature dropped well below freezing it was so cold in the courtyard that those with thinner clothes were directed into the hall while those who could afford warmer clothes were asked to sit in the frigid courtyard, often in the snow. Finally in 1936, the church saved enough money to buy some property and build a church, which they named "The Christian Tabernacle." It seated up to eight hundred persons and was regularly filled to capacity at the regular services on Sundays as well as those held during the week.[29]

Wang's demand for simplicity affected all aspects of the Christian Tabernacle. He was to be addressed simply as "Mr. Wang Mingdao." There was no choir because Wang felt they distracted from the preaching of the Word and served as mere entertainment. Collections were never taken. Instead, a box was placed outside the sanctuary to collect gifts anonymously. Later Wang recalled:

> The equipment and furnishings inside the hall were marked by simplicity, cleanliness and dignity. The walls were as white as snow and no words or pictures were hung on them. This was so that nothing should distract the attention of the worshippers so that they could worship God with singleness of heart. Neither outside the building nor inside did we have a cross. . . . A white stone on the southeast corner carries an inscription of four sentences which indicate our faith and the truths we emphasize. . . . "He was wounded for our transgressions. He rose again from the dead. He has already been received into heaven. He will come again to receive us."[30]

Evidence of regeneration, signified by "the change in [one's] manner of life," was necessary for baptism. Consequently, some waited as long as one or two years before being baptized. The church had no salaried workers. Moreover, the criteria for workers in the church were "belief" and "integrity," whereas "gifts . . . power . . . knowledge and learning were considered secondary."[31]

As noted earlier, Wang deplored the deference shown to the wealthy and powerful. Thus, wealth, fame, or power curried no favor or notoriety at the Christian Tabernacle. Although on occasion the affluent and influential did attend, few stayed for long. Such departures didn't distress Wang: "Some onlookers would regard this as our church's loss, but in actual fact it is our gain. For where you have vain people who love vain-glory in a church it means a very great handicap for the church."[32]

On the other hand, faith and personal integrity were highly valued. Wang remarked, "In my ministry I emphasize the faith of believers, and the moral life of believers. On the one hand I preach the important truth of the Bible, while at the same time I preach on the moral teaching of the Bible."[33] Even his detractors knew of and respected the discipline his church embodied as well as Wang's own personal integrity. Whereas other independent evangelicals such as Watchman Nee and Isaac Wei would be arrested after 1949 on ethics and corruption charges, Wang Mingdao's unwavering commitment to personal and ecclesial integrity made him a difficult person to impugn.

The Christian Tabernacle was congregational and avoided any official institutional relationship with other churches or foreign missionary organizations. Wang did not regard the members of his church to be the only true followers of Christ; rather, independence was sought to ensure sound doctrine and proper discipline. This independence also freed his hand to accomplish what he saw as his personal vocation and the vocation of the church to be a prophetic witness to both church and world. In Wang's words:

I have no desire to do something great. It is simply my hope, in this world where truth is beclouded and where the lusts of men have broken their banks, to be able to testify to God's truth and to live out His life. I wanted to be faithful unto death; in my own particular sphere I want to glorify God; and I want to spread the fragrance of Christ wherever I go. It is not so much a large church that I want to build; it is rather to build up a church according to the mind of God. Two needs stand out in the world today. One is for model believers; the other is for model churches. My prayer accordingly, is that we may be model believers, and that ours may be a model church.[34]

Independent in ministry, finances, and mission, Wang consistently refused all institutional and foreign entanglements. This independent stance would make it difficult in years to come to tar him with the brush of Western imperialism.

Confronting the Japanese

Japanese incursions into China in the late 1930s led to large areas of northern and central China including Beijing falling under Japanese control. Keen to cut off Western influence and ensure Chinese cooperation with their rule, the Japanese initially closed all churches with foreign mission ties and funding. To reopen, these churches had to join the North China Christian Federation established to unify all Protestant churches within a single denomination.

Wang at first ignored the invitation to join this new union. He saw no need to have anything to do with it because his church had no foreign connections. Subsequent pressure to join, however, was soon applied as letters demanding his attendance at meetings of the Federation were received at the church. He replied to the Federation:

> I acknowledge the receipt of your letter directing me to join the North China Christian Federation Promotion Committee. On examining your statement with its references to Western Missions and to the objective of becoming self-supporting, self-governing and self-propagating, I conclude that it is not necessary for us to join your group. In addition to that your Federation is made up of churches of different faiths from ours and in order to preserve an unadulterated faith it would be difficult for us to affiliate with churches of different faiths. Consequently we are unable to follow your directions and send a representative to your meeting. I hope you will understand our position.[35]

In 1939, the Japanese sent an order requiring all journals and newspapers published in Beijing to include the official seal of the Japanese Army Bureau, which included four slogans supporting Japanese occupation.[36] Because these slogans did not represent his views or those of his church, Wang believed it would be wrong to allow them in his journal. Nonetheless, he felt duty-bound to continue printing and distributing the *Spiritual Food Quarterly*. Although fearful that he might be arrested, he submitted the journal without the seal as well as his subscription list to the authorities. Surprisingly, the Japanese officials made no response, and the journal was approved and sent without the required seal.

Finally, Wang was summoned to the office of a Mr. Takeda, the investigating officer of the North China Cultural Bureau, which had been set up to oversee the churches. Takeda warned Wang that the policy of union would be carried out by force, if necessary. Wang replied that his church would "pay any price, and make any sacrifice" necessary to uphold their beliefs.[37] Takeda allowed him to leave, but Wang feared imminent arrest. Even Wang's friends in the church urged him to compromise. As one friend put it: "Are you not aware that for the Japanese military to kill a Chinese is no more than our killing an ant?" Wang replied, "What you say is correct, but I am not an ant. I am the servant of the most high God. Unless God permits, no one can harm me."[38]

In the end, the Japanese took no action against Wang Mingdao or his church. Wang took this as divine providence as well as confirmation of God's protection of those like himself who were unwilling to bend in order to preserve the integrity and independence of the church. It only strengthened his resolve to resist all entanglements that might compromise his principles and faith. It also helps explain Wang's refusal to join the patriotic union of churches after the Communist revolution a decade later. Though governments might threaten, when faced with a principled stand they would never follow through on their threats.

The first half of the twentieth century was a period of unprecedented social and cultural upheaval in China. That turmoil, however, also allowed for an equally unprecedented amount of spiritual and religious autonomy for figures such as Wang Mingdao. In a social situation that lacked stable governmental authority, Wang's independence, congregationalism, and resistance to official ties with other Protestant churches were generally ignored. That began to change with Japanese pressure to unify Protestantism in Beijing, but it would change radically after Mao's victorious armies marched into Beijing in 1949.

THREE

Joining the United Front

The Church and the Chinese Communist Party

Communists may form an anti-imperialist and anti-feudal united-front for political action with certain idealists and even with religious followers, but we can never approve of their idealism or religious doctrines.[1]

Mao Zedong (1940)

The relative peace Wang Mingdao and his church had enjoyed before Japanese occupation returned with their defeat and departure in 1945. This tranquillity, however, was short-lived. The Communist Revolution was gathering force in the countryside and would soon inundate all of China and forever change the nation, the church, and the lives of those caught up in its turbulent path. For the people of Beijing, the three years between the departure of the Japanese and the arrival of the Communists were a strange alchemy of survival, wonder, dread, and hope. They observed anxiously as the foreigners and missionaries who had only so recently returned now melted away with the Chiang Kai-shek's fleeing Nationalist forces as they abandoned China's ancient capital to the advancing Liberation Army.

What this "liberation" held in store no one knew for sure; what was certain was that life under the Communists would be radically different.

With Mao and his victorious armies came the dawn of "New China."[2] The plan of Mao and the Communist Party was to forge a modern and mighty nation out of the disparate factions of Chinese society. Drawing upon the ancient Chinese ideal of social and political harmony, Mao and the Communist Party would put their ideological stamp upon society. It is only as we come to grasp the nature of that imposition upon the church that we can come to understand the stiff resistance of Wang Mingdao and the bitter conflict that erupted soon after.

Unity in Search of a Modern Nation

The pursuit of social, moral, and political unity is ancient in China. The term *Datong* ("grand unity") can be found in the earliest written records of the empire. More than an ideal, the *Datong* was the yardstick by which empires and emperors, revolutions and revolutionaries were measured. The *Datong* was the wisdom, strength, peace, and harmony that distanced the empire from the rancor and division that led to weakness, chaos, war, and death.

For nearly two millennia China's *Datong* had found its center in the monarch seated upon the dragon throne. By the twentieth century, however, foreigners from without and corruption from within had decimated China's *Datong*. Foreigners bled China by means of withering indemnities for past conflicts and unequal treaties that confiscated her lucrative ports. From within, bandits, warlords, and greedy officials carved out sections of the empire as personal fiefdoms, leaving the nation weak and subject to her enemies. By 1912 the empire collapsed of its own weight as the child emperor Pu Yi abdicated, "bowing to the 'Mandate of Heaven'... manifested through the wish of the people."[3]

The demise of the monarchy led Confucians, nationalists, fascists, and Communists to pursue a new *Datong* that would remove China's disgrace, restore her lands, and secure her place among the nations of the world. As several factions joined together to form a new republic, General Yuan Shi-kai, secured the presidency in 1912 by outmaneuvering Dr. Sun Yat-sen, the intellectual force behind the nationalist revolution of 1911. Nonetheless, General Yuan's tenuous grip on power soon gave way and the nation divided into warring camps between 1916 and 1928.

In 1917, Sun Yat-sen reemerged and by 1923 had begun to forge a strategic alliance of his Kuomintang (Nationalist Party) with the fledgling Communist Party. Sun then set about establishing the Kuomintang army under the command of General Chiang Kai-shek to break the power of the warlords who divided China and left her subject to the whims of Western nations. The alliance with the Communists, however, was short-lived. Not only did each side distrust the other, they actively competed with each other to swing the loyalty of the combined army their way. Sun Yat-sen's unexpected death in 1925 shattered what little remained of this fragile alliance. Moving to fill this vacuum, Chiang Kai-shek seized power and moved to exterminate the Communists. By 1927, Chiang had destroyed most of the armed wing of the Communist Party. Between 1931 and 1934 Chiang attempted to finish the job with four bloody campaigns. Facing certain extinction if they remained, an estimated 100,000 Communist Party members and sympathizers fled central China on a six-thousand-mile trek across China under constant military harassment to the wilderness of Yenan. Here the 20,000 survivors would establish a base beyond the reach of Chiang's army. In the years to come they would heal their wounds, swell their ranks, and elevate the brilliant and charismatic Mao Zedong as their leader.

Japan's full-scale invasion of China in 1937 suspended the conflict between the Nationalists and the Communists, as they now turned on their common foe Japan. With Chiang's attention directed toward the Japanese, the Communist armies were able to hone their tactics against the Japanese to defeat a foe with superior troop strength and weaponry. The surrender of the Japanese in 1945 allowed Chiang to once again direct his sites on the Communists. With three million troops equipped with superior American weaponry, victory for the Kuomintang army seemed assured. Nonetheless, lack of a compelling political vision, petty jealousies between commanders, the loss of precious supplies and ammunition due to pilfering by corrupt officers, and the growing lack of confidence of Kuomintang soldiers for their officers led to devastating defeats in the field. As arms and men fell into the hands of the advancing Communist troops, Chiang's early defeats gave way to a full scale rout and Chiang was forced to flee to Taiwan even as Mao's victorious armies marched into Beijing unhindered.

With the Communist victory a century of humiliation had come to an end, and Mao could now ascend the Gate of Heavenly Peace (Tiananmen) and proclaim to the exultant masses that "the Chinese People have stood up." China's *Datong* had been restored, in Mao's words, by "a well disciplined Party armed with the theory of Marxist-Leninism, an army under the leadership of such a party, and a united-front of all revolutionary classes and all revolutionary groups."[4] This united front was no mere alliance. Encompassing both an ideology, a policy, and an institution, the united front allowed the Communist Party to marshal sympathetic and even hostile forces to assist in its meteoric rise to power. Now the ideology, policy, and institution of the united front would be put to use to forge a nation out of the feuding factions that had divided China for nearly half a century.

Christians and the Revolution

China's one million Protestants in 1949 were but a drop in China's vast sea of over five hundred million souls. Seeing China fall into the hands of Mao and the Communists only heightened the sense of insignificance and insecurity for most Christians. How would the Communists treat Christians? Would those who had publicly opposed the Communists be imprisoned or executed? Would churches be allowed to remain open? What would happen to relationships with foreign missions and missionaries? How would Communist ideology affect theology, Christian identity, and church union?

The Communist Party, for its part, had its own anxieties about the influence of Christians in society. Though small in actual numbers,

Christians represented a significant percentage of the educated work-force. As doctors, administrators, skilled technicians, and teachers, they ran the hospitals, colleges, and other institutions established by missionary organizations, which needed to continue operating if the new political order was to proceed smoothly.

This posed a dilemma for the Communists, for as much as they needed the Christians to help run the country, they knew that many resented the Communist Party. Not only were the Communists athe-ists, Christians and Communists had had a stormy relationship well before the revolution. In the 1920s, the Communist Party had been at the forefront of anti-Christian propaganda. Grisly tales of the deaths of Christians and missionaries at the hands of the Communists before and during the revolution were a source of fear, anger, and distrust. In turn, the Communists had viewed Christianity as an ideological rival and a political threat given the backing of highly placed West-ern missionary leaders for the regime of Chiang Kai-shek.

With Christians represented in key sectors throughout society, they represented a necessary evil that the Communists would have to deal with wisely. As Mao himself acknowledged:

> the reactionary forces in the missionary schools established in China by the imperialists and in religious circles and those in the cultural and education institutions . . . These are our enemies we have to fight them one and all. . . . This is a very acute struggle unprecedented in history.[5]

To secure loyalty, to root out the Party's enemies, and to ensure national stability, Mao applied the strategy that had won the war: a "united front" that would recognize those loyal to the Party while iso-lating their foes.

The United Front: From Successful Strategy to Latent Ideology

The Chinese Communist Party (CCP) has always represented just a fraction of China's massive population. Thus, from its inception, the Party required strategic alliances with non-Communists to survive, expand, and eventually take power. The ideological and institutional glue that held these alliances together was known as the "united front." A united front was formed wherever like interest or a common enemy allowed beneficial alliances with non-Communists.

The term *united front* was originally adopted from Marxist ideology. Its purpose was to organize society into various categories so that the working class could take advantage of common concerns to unite against common class enemies and thus vanquish them one at a time. An inner-Party directive explained, "In the struggle against the anti-Communist diehards, we must take advantage of their contradictions in order to win over the majority, oppose the minority, and crush the enemies separately; it is a line of justifiability, expediency, and restraint."[6]

Eschewing the rigid class distinctions found within the Soviet Union, the CCP used categories that were elastic and suited the situation at any given moment. Thus, when it came to distinguishing friend from foe, relative sympathy or hostility toward the CCP was far more important than rigid class distinctions. As the Party's needs changed, so did the united front. It evolved over time from a military tactic to a political strategy to the national policy of the People's Republic of China even as the Party was transformed from a rebel band hiding in the caves of Yenan to the ruling party in Beijing.[7]

The United Front as a Form of Political Control

To understand how the united front functioned *politically*, one must understand Mao's "theory of contradictions." According to this theory, society progresses through various stages by overcoming social, political, or economic conflict, the so-called "contradictions" in Marxist rhetoric. Overcoming contradictions is a historical and political process by which society evolves from feudalism to capitalism to socialism and eventually to communism as the forces of revolution, *the left*, come into conflict with reactionary forces opposed to revolution, *the right*. The struggle between these antithetical forces creates contradictions that are overcome through a progressive political synthesis, a united front, that overcomes the social and political contradictions of any given age. Accordingly, the CCP represented and led this united front in that it had to struggle against both doctrinaire Marxists on the *left* who sought to impose a rigid Marxist orthodoxy on society as well as the forces of reaction on the *right* that sought to overturn the revolution. Only through struggle with both *right* and *left* contradictions could the Party ensure the stable progress of the revolution in a strong united front.

In China, primarily an agrarian nation, the revolution had already overcome the first major contradiction between feudalism and nationalism, since most major landlords had fled or been killed and their lands distributed into government-run communes. Consequently, attention was turned to the far more difficult contradiction between the political leadership of the CCP and the urban, educated classes of China. These classes were needed to manage the bureaucratic infrastructure required for social reconstruction, so mass imprisonment and execution would have been counterproductive. Thus, the principle contradiction between the CCP and the non-Communist educated classes was broken down into two types of contradictions. Non-Communist parties, groups, affiliations, and individuals who could be brought around to accepting and working under the leadership of the CCP were labeled *nonantagonistic contradictions*. This type of contradiction could be overcome through discussion, criticism, persuasion, and indoctrination.[8] Those who could neither work with nor accept the leadership of the CCP were labeled *antagonistic contradictions*. These were regarded as the incorrigible enemies of the people and were subject to arrest, public humiliation, imprisonment, or even execution.

Mao's theory of contradictions assumed that, at any given time, 6 to 10 percent of the population represented *antagonistic contradictions* who needed to be ferreted out and eliminated.[9] As a result, the line of demarcation between loyal citizen and "enemy of the people" was in a constant state of flux based on the whims of the Party at any given moment. Continual realignment of who represented antagonistic contradictions served its purpose by keeping the populace in a state of anxiety. Those caught in this anxiety could easily be leveraged by means of their fear of being labeled "an enemy of the people." Applied carefully, pressure could be brought to bear on the non-Communist "wavering middle" to ensure Party loyalty.

United Front as Institution

To secure the loyalty of the non-Communists needed to run the country, the CCP established the United Front Work Department (UFWD) in 1949. The UFWD served as the communication bridge between the government and the people, disseminating official policy, monitoring compliance, and reporting back to the Party leadership. As an organ of social and political control, its means to achieve these ends were rigorous surveillance and ideological remolding. Surveillance was detailed, continuous, and omnipresent:

> Every day (agents of the UFWD and other party departments) collect and send in large amounts of intelligence (on people) ranging from the leaders of the various parties, such as Li Chi-shen and Huang Yen-pe'i down to small fry in cultural circles living in little inns outside the Ch'ien-men (main gate); no one is exempted from surveillance, investigation and report.[10]

The UFWD kept tabs on all non-Communist organizations by attending all meetings, ensuring that all financial resources were accounted for and approved by the UFWD, maintaining dossiers on all individuals or groups, and ensuring mandatory attendance at the regular political indoctrination sessions.

Ideological remolding was the second tool at the UFWD's disposal to ensure compliance with Party leadership. During the war years, the CCP required all members to attend intense thought-reform sessions. During these sessions members were encouraged to expose faults and errant ideas through self-criticism or by denouncing them in others. In this manner feudal or imperialist residue could be exposed and purged. Referred to as "denunciation" sessions or "accusation meetings," they could last for days, often focusing on a single individual. Of critical importance was to get close friends and family members to accuse the individual so that his or her "crimes" would come to the surface and be recognized, thus producing a catharsis whereby all non-proletarian thought could be eliminated. After this purification process, the members received reeducation to instill revolutionary ideology. Yu Ting-ying explained, "Purity of thought consciousness is a matter of inserting proletarian thought-consciousness with self-awareness into the brain and continually overcoming and cleaning up all non-proletarian thought consciousness in the brain. This kind of purity amounts to being in an awakened state."[11]

Thought reform was not new to China, but the intensity, nature, and extent of thought reform across the entire nation under the Communist Party was unprecedented. Should crimes surface during these interrogation sessions, individuals could be arrested, imprisoned, or executed. It was not uncommon for people to commit suicide rather than to face the shame and humiliation of being disgraced or seeing one's family members pressured into being one's chief accusers.

The United Front Work Department and Religious Policy

Even before the revolution, the CCP had sought to influence Christian organizations that might be sympathetic to its cause. As with other non-Communist parties and institutions, part of the united front policy of the CCP was to infiltrate Christian organizations with secret Communist Party operatives. Their job was to probe these institutions to discover possible alliances, but also to flag those that represented *antagonistic contradictions.*

Though up to 1949, evangelical groups had largely thwarted CCP penetration, CCP attempts to infiltrate their organizations angered evangelicals and heightened their suspicion of CCP activity in more liberal Christian groups. Evangelicals suspected key leaders in the liberal YMCA and YWCA were not merely sympathetic to the Communists but were secret Communist Party members.[12] As a result, evangelicals were not surprised later when these leaders were called upon by the government to establish a patriotic union of all Protestant churches in China.

Resistance to the CCP was not limited to evangelicals. A significant group of more liberal Protestant missionaries and Christians had actively supported Chiang Kai-shek. Chiang's wife, daughter of a banker, power-broker, and former finance minister of the Kuomintang,

T. V. Soong, had been active in soliciting the support of Western Christians for the Chiang regime. Those who had hoped that Chiang would establish a Christian nation were bitterly disappointed when he failed and represented some of the Communist Party's most bitter enemies. They viewed Marxism and atheism as the foundation of tyranny and the antithesis of Christian democracy and human liberty.

Finally, at the other end of the spectrum were the Christians who actively supported the Communists, or at least saw their rule as a vast improvement over that of Chiang Kai-shek. These Christians saw in the agrarian reform and promotion of the peasant cause by the Communist Party the type of social reconstruction they had longed prayed for. Enthusiasm for the Communist revolution was particularly marked among young Christian intellectuals who were part of the "Christian Movement," whose numbers were largely found in the YMCA and the YWCA. This group of young Christian intellectuals saw in the Communist Party's social and economic reform the vindication of the Social Gospel and the manifestation of the kingdom of God on earth.[13] Accordingly, they argued, the church should actively support the CCP and the establishment of a "New China."

Thus, at the founding of the People's Republic of China, Protestants and their churches represented the very sort of mixed contradiction that required sorting out by the UFWD. The rapid expansion of Christian missions into China's interior in the mid-twentieth century had dispersed Christians widely throughout China. Since Christians were no longer isolated in small pockets near major cities, the UFWD was faced with a massive, complicated task. Moreover, official and unofficial church networks connected Christians not only throughout China but also in nations hostile to the Communist Party. Finally, money from Western missionary agencies gave Christians a measure of independence from government manipulation or coercion.

The United Front and the Churches of China

In 1949, as part of the overall strategy of the united front, the Communist Party invited delegates from non-Communist parties to endorse a tentative constitution at the Chinese People's Political Consultative Conference (CPPCC). The document drafted at the conference set forth the "Common Program," which spelled out the agenda for non-Communist parties to join the united front under the leadership of the Communist Party in order to establish the new nation. The delegates to the CPPCC were then commissioned to establish patriotic organizations to work with and facilitate the work of the UFWD.

Four official delegates from the Protestant churches attended: Y. T. Wu, Cora Deng (YWCA National Secretary), T. C. Chao, and Zhang Xue-yan (editor of the *Christian Forum*). All were prominent Christians known for their outspoken support for the CCP and the Christian Movement.[14] Their charge was the successful incorporation of Protestant Christians into the united front both ideologically and institutionally.

After the conference in Beijing, their first task was to fan out across the country to calm the fears of Christians by communicating the government's religious policy. According to the constitution, freedom of religious belief and worship were guaranteed. Moreover, if at any place revolutionary zeal had wrongly impinged on stated policy, this was to be reported to the relevant authorities, who would rectify the situation. Teams were thus set up to visit churches and to "explain and promote the policy of religious freedom; and to deepen cooperation and understanding between Church and government leaders in local areas."[15]

The United Front and Indigenous Christian Movements

Although religious belief was officially guaranteed for the masses, two groups were immediately singled out as "enemies of the people." The first, as might be expected, included those who had been closely aligned with the Chiang regime or who had been closely associated with foreign missionaries. Thus Bishop W. Y. Chen, who had close relations with Chiang, was arrested in 1951. Anglican Bishop Kimber Den and Baen Lee, the latter a scholar with the Church of Christ in China, were also arrested but were later released when the government admitted that their imprisonment was in error.[16] A few, rather than be subject to the shame of denunciation, arrest, and imprisonment, committed suicide.[17] Needless to say, these high-profile cases sent shock waves through the Christian community and convinced most denominational leaders to submit to reeducation and to participate in the united front.

The second group of Christians targeted were independent indigenous churches and their leaders. Representing nearly a quarter of all Protestants in China in 1949, these movements had no ties with Western missionary organizations, were self-sufficient, and were funded by the donations of members or simply held all things in common. In spite of their independence from foreign involvement, these groups were hounded by the nation-state after 1949.

The leaders of the Jesus Family, the True Jesus Church, and the Little Flock were all arrested and imprisoned and their churches broken up. Some of their members joined more traditional churches, while others began to meet clandestinely and thus were subject to harassment and arrest. The largest of these indigenous movements was Watchman Nee's Little Flock. Founded in the 1920s as a result of Nee's evangelistic crusades, the Little Flock established nearly one thousand local churches and, by 1949, claimed ninety thousand followers.[18] Initially, Nee tried to work with the government, but in 1951 he was arrested. Of the long list of charges against Nee, which included everything from embezzlement to rape, the only charge that has ever been substantiated was the charge of taking church funds for his own purposes. This took place before the CCP came to power and had been resolved by Nee and the church.[19]

Why the CCP went after the indigenous independent Christian movements is an interesting question. Since they were independent of Western churches and missionaries, they represented no security threat. Their members were not educated and strategically placed Christians, so there was no need for the government to secure their support to keep social services functioning. Nonetheless, what appears to be the common denominator that attracted the negative attention of the government was their independence and heterodox views. Their financial independence allowed them to ignore the dictates of the UFWD, and their theological idiosyncrasies made union with other Protestants unlikely. Thus, they complicated the desire of the government to bring the Protestant churches into the united front. Moreover, unlike Wang Mingdao, these churches and their leaders had little support outside their own groups. Theologically, their views were heterodox leading more orthodox pastors and churches to view them as dangerous sects and cults. As a result they were exclusive, viewing their churches as the only authentic representative of Christianity in China, which, in turn, led to aggressive tactics to lure Christians away from other churches. Thus, the suppression of these churches and the arrest of their leaders created little stir among Christians in China; indeed, many were glad to see them removed.

The Christian Manifesto and the United Front

In 1950 Y. T. Wu requested a meeting of select Protestant leaders with the prime minister, Zhou Enlai. Zhou encouraged Wu to form a committee to draft a document that would provide the blueprint for the future of Protestantism in China in light of the realities of the new government and the political leadership of the Communist Party. The document the committee drafted, entitled "The Christian Manifesto," was submitted to Zhou for his approval. With Zhou's approval and bearing the signatures of forty Christian leaders, the Manifesto was published with a front-page endorsement in the national newspaper, the *People's Daily*. Shortly thereafter official delegations were sent to churches throughout China with the Manifesto in hand to secure the signatures of Protestants in support of the Christian Manifesto.

The gathering of signatures, dubbed the "Three-Self Reform Movement," marked the beginning of the establishment of a union of Protestant churches under the banner of patriotism and anti-imperialism. The Christian Manifesto was the charter document of this union, the Three-Self Reform Movement its institution.[20]

Although the Christian Manifesto mentions no author, the style and content of the document point to Y. T. Wu as its principal draftsman.[21] The Manifesto is divided into four sections (see appendix 1). The first section retells the history of Protestantism in China, revealing the role of imperialism in the Christian missionary enterprise. Over time, the Manifesto maintains, Chinese Christians consciously and subconsciously accepted imperialism, which they eventually confused with the gospel itself. Thus, Christians in China needed to be reformed to prevent the enemies of China from using "Christianity to forward their plot of stirring up internal dissension, and creating reactionary forces in this country."[22] The Manifesto goes on to state:

> Now that the Chinese revolution has achieved victory, these imperialistic countries will not rest passively content in face of this unprecedented historical fact in China. They will certainly seek to contrive by every means the destruction of what has actually been achieved; they may also make use of Christianity to forward their plot of stirring up internal dissension and creating reactionary forces in this country. *It is our purpose in publishing the following statement to heighten our vigilance against imperialism, to make known the clear political stand of Christians in New China.*[23]

The second section addressed what needed to be done to fight this imperialist threat. Like other non-Communist organizations and parties of the united front, Protestant churches were required to support the "Common Political Platform" and the leadership of the Communist Party. Further, Christians, as patriotic citizens, were to participate in the construction of an "independent, democratic, peaceable, unified, prosperous, and powerful New China." Several concrete steps were to be taken by Protestant churches in this regard. They were to instill vigilance against "imperialism" in their members, to sever ties with all foreign organizations and subsidies in "the shortest time possible," and to become Three-Self churches: self supporting, self-governing, and self-propagating (hence the name Three-Self Reform Movement).[24]

The Three-Self principles were not new. Missionaries at the end of the nineteenth century had advocated these principles as the goal of their missionary work, which was to establish independent and indigenous churches in China. Nonetheless, given the argument of the Christian Manifesto, it was obvious that the political concerns of the UFWD far outweighed traditional missiological concerns. Self-government cut off foreign influence and interference. Self-support—that is, the end of foreign subsidies—meant not only financial independence from foreign institutions but also greater material dependence on the government. Finally, self-propagation required the message and mission of the church to be reformed so that it dovetailed with government plans to remold all the citizens ideologically. In short, by taking the title of the Three-Self Reform Movement, the process of bringing all Protestants into a single manageable entity could be championed as the realization of the great ends of the establishment of an independent Chinese church.

That the parameters of the Three-Self Church were forged in accord with the interests of the Communist Party can be seen in the troubles the Communist Party had with the Catholic Church. Pressure was applied early on to establish a Patriotic Catholic Church that would sever ties with the Vatican and become self-governing, self-supporting, and self-propagating. However, the government's attempt to enlist Chinese priests to form a new hierarchy failed miserably. The handful they were able to woo found themselves cut off from the Roman Catholic Church, since mass was withheld from any who advocated severance with Rome. Further, the church officially denounced thought reform and forbade Catholics from active involvement in the security, military, or political branches of the government.[25]

The Communist Party responded by deporting Inter-Nuncio Cardinal Riberi in 1951, imprisoning a significant number of priests, and seizing church properties. In spite of this pressure, the Chinese bishops refused to budge. For several years the Catholic Church successfully rebuffed every government attempt to force them into a patriotic united front and to cut off ties with the Vatican. Finally, however, the government forcibly took over the Catholic churches in 1955 in its campaign to "eliminate the counter-revolutionaries in the Catholic Church."[26] The bishop of Shanghai was arrested, as well as most of the priesthood throughout the country. Though this campaign effectively crushed Catholic resistance, it was a hollow victory. So many priests had been imprisoned that the church could no longer administer the sacraments in all its dioceses. An empty shell, the Chinese

Catholic Patriotic Association was made up of only a handful of priests who were forced to serve in the new institution. Loyalty remained with Rome even if that sentiment no longer was allowed an official voice in China. To this day, the tension between the Roman Catholic Church and the CCP is palpable. An estimated eight million Catholics are in the underground Catholic Church. The Vatican recognizes its own priesthood and even consecrated the Bishop of Shanghai as a Cardinal *in absentia* even as he served his life sentence at a government labor camp.

The Theology of the Christian Manifesto

In light of the events above, it is not surprising that both supporters and detractors of the Three-Self Reform Movement have viewed the Christian Manifesto as a political document rather than a theological document. While some have regarded it as a political betrayal of the church, others have held it up as a practical document that provided a necessary blueprint for Christian existence in an avowedly Marxist society. Unfortunately, viewing the Christian Manifesto primarily in political terms has blinded commentators to the theological ramifications of the document and of the Three-Self Reform Movement. That it is a theological as well as a political document can be seen in the influence of its principal architect, Y. T. Wu.

Leading up to the revolution, Y. T. Wu charged that Protestantism had come to view itself "above ideologies, and above nations and times."[27] This, according to Wu, led to a type of "ineffectual reformism" that tried to improve, rather than replace, bankrupt political and economic systems. Such "reformism" had left the church out of step with the "ruthless judgment of history." Because Protestantism, in Wu's view, had opposed historical progress, it had gone from a "conservative force" merely holding back progress to a "reactionary force" actively fighting against it. Thus Wu charged Protestantism with being unfaithful to its revolutionary roots. True Christianity had to return to the "pure gospel" of welcoming the "judgment of history" found in the revolution and in the establishment of "New China."[28]

The Christian Manifesto reflected Wu's view that the Spirit of God should be discerned in social and political progress. Wu agreed with the Marxists that society progresses through intermediate stages inexorably toward a just and peaceful society. However, such progress only had meaning if it participated in the divine ideal of the perfect society. Consequently, Wu argued that Marxist materialism and theism should not be opposed; rather, socialist transformation of the nation toward a classless and just society and the Christian construction of the kingdom of God should be seen as one. Here one can see that the Manifesto's political concern to establish a Protestant union within a patriotic united front was theological. It sought to reform the church to accord with the progressive ideology of the Communist Party so that it might keep pace with the God of history now manifest in the revolutionary movement sweeping the world. Given the theological predisposition of the Christian Manifesto it is not surprising that years later Y. T. Wu would propose to Li Weihan, a key leader of the CCP Central Committee, that the state should adopt "socialist religion" as the spiritual framework of the nation.[29] Though this suggestion was dismissed by Li Weihan, it reveals Wu's position reflected in the Manifesto that religion and national progress were cut from the same spiritual cloth.

Whereas the Christian Manifesto set out the program for the churches, the Three-Self Reform Movement carried it out. The first order of business was to secure the support of Chinese Protestants by having them endorse the Christian Manifesto. The outbreak of the Korean War made this job much easier. With Chinese troops engaged in Korea against American troops, signing the Christian Manifesto expressed loyalty to the nation in the face of the enemy. Although the Christian Manifesto had initially "encountered obstruction" and resistance, it now gathered momentum, so that by 1953 it had been signed by nearly 400,000 Christians—nearly half the Protestant population in China at that time.[30]

The Three-Self Reform Movement's charge to sever the ties of foreign missions with Chinese churches was already complete before the signature drive began, with nearly all Protestant missionaries having left China by 1951. Thus began the more difficult work to purge the imperialist influence the missionaries had left behind in the conscious and unconscious attitudes of Chinese Christians. The war in Korea only added impetus to purify the churches of this "imperialist poison." This would begin as part of the "Resist America Aid Korea Three-Self Movement" instigated by the Three-Self Movement as evidence of their patriotic zeal. The goal was to "finally, completely, and totally cut off links with American and other missions in order to achieve self-government, self-propagation, and self-support for all Chinese churches."[31]

Ideological Remolding and the Denunciation Movement

Anxiety among Chinese Christians ran high at this time. With the CCP still working to establish its position in China, open trials, mass arrests, and public executions were common. With the Korean conflict in full swing, there was increased pressure on Christians to show their opposition to America and imperialism as well as their solidarity with the government. To that end, ideological remolding sessions within Christian organizations began in earnest. They began with groups that strongly endorsed the Christian Manifesto and the Three-Self Reform Movement. The National Christian Council, YMCA, YWCA, and the Christian Literature Society all carried out denunciation meetings. Subsequently, flyers were distributed to Christian organizations and churches throughout the country with instructions as to how to hold their own successful "accusation meetings."[32]

At these denunciation meetings, Christians were encouraged to renounce all connection with Western imperialism and to confess their complicity in foreign aggression. This denunciation was at once ideological and personal. The object was not just to confess one's sins but to target "imperialist elements and their helpers... hidden in the Church." Initially, those targeted for denunciation were those who had had close relationships with foreign missionaries ("imperialist elements"). Normally these were denominational leaders or those in schools, hospitals, and other charitable organizations who had had close contact with the Western Protestant missionaries before they had left China. These individuals would be led into a hall where workers and colleagues were gathered to denounce them. Private sentiment was not to hinder the denunciation; rather, the accusers were to "break through all sentimentality." According to one document of this period, "The general approach was for the speaker to identify the individual being criticized as an agent or 'running dog' of American imperialism; substantiate the charge with particular examples or evidence; and provide a self-criticism for one's own complicity in the relationship."[33]

The expressed purpose of these denunciations was to "wipe out the influences of imperialism" so that patriotic consciousness could be instilled. Certainly this approach was taken for political reasons, but once again it had theological, spiritual ramifications. If one reads through recorded confessions, one discovers a consistent pattern whereby political ideology confronted and then transformed traditional Christian belief so that the latter was in accord with the more fundamental ideological narrative. One Christian confessed:

> I have had over 30 years of experience as a pastor of the Church. . . . In the past I always took the attitude of "standing aloof from the world" and "covering up others' bad deeds while praising their virtues." . . . I discovered the error of that kind of thinking, which is that it is in no way beneficial to the nation. Leniency towards enemies is cruelty to oneself. . . . I came to a deep awareness of the pain and ideological struggle, and the joy which follows. From the Christian perspective, I can say that from that day on, I found new life.[34]

In this confession we see traditional Christian language transformed. Enlightenment, conviction, conversion, regeneration, joy, and salvation all appear, to be sure, but they are defined or given meaning in terms of the nation, not Christ or the church.

This spiritual and theological reform had, of course, certain emphases. One particular error that needed to be overcome was leniency toward enemies, which had led to less than enthusiastic participation in ideological campaigns to root out the nation's enemies.

Some Christian ideas, such as "love your enemies," "do not kill people," "Christians do not belong to this world," and "forgive people seventy times seven times," were used . . . to oppose the anti-imperialist patriotic struggles . . . *causing some Christians to blur the line between themselves and their enemies and hindering their progress in patriotism.* Patriotic Christian figures, again drawing on the Bible, held that all religious concepts must be understood in an all-around way, using the Bible as background for linking all beliefs. They pointed out that believers according to the teachings of Jesus, should distinguish right from wrong, good from bad, and should oppose evil forces, plunging themselves into the cause of just struggles. The imperialists and reactionaries inside the Church had committed many evil acts that brought harm to the motherland and the people. *To apply mechanistically the teachings of "love your enemies" and "do not kill people" and let them do what they want would be a sin against Christian moral teachings.*[35]

Once again, the latent theology of the Christian Manifesto is evident. Because the progress of the "motherland" is divine, sin is the failure to denounce, exclude, and punish the enemies of the state. Righteousness, on the other hand, is the "plunging . . . into the cause of just struggles." In this manner, the common ground of the united front served as the political and theological backdrop by which one was properly to interpret Scripture. In the end, no tension was allowed to exist between Christianity and the state, for the gospel simply affirmed the united front.

For the CCP, "instilling correct thinking in people's minds" was a necessary step in China's progress.[36] Moreover, only those Chinese Christians who were willing to "draw a line" between themselves and their imperialist roots and to reveal their solidarity with the new order could be trusted.[37] Many have argued that because such ideological remolding was political and ideological, resistance on the part of Christians such as Wang Mingdao was unnecessary. Such a view is naïve, for the adoption of the Common Platform, incorporation into the united front, signing on to the Christian Manifesto, and becoming part of the Three-Self Reform Movement all had theological and spiritual ramifications. This movement understood Christian faith according to a radically different gospel, according to a significantly different narrative than has been traditionally associated with ortho-dox Christianity. In this manner the Communist Party's narrative of China overwhelmed the church and transformed its gospel politi-cally, spiritually, and theologically.

Consolidation and Institution of the Three-Self Patriotic Movement

As the de facto organizational bridge between the UFWD and Protestant churches from 1950 until 1954, the Three-Self Reform Movement still lacked official status. Sanction by the Protestant church nationwide and official recognition by the UFWD was required if it was to become an official organization under the UFWD. To rec-tify this situation, 232 delegates were summoned to Beijing to adopt a constitution that would legitimize the formal institution of the Three-Self Reform Movement.

Conservatives, however, were reluctant. They believed that the use of the term *reform* suggested that they were reforming their beliefs. In order to address this objection, a compromise was struck. It was agreed that the name be changed to the Three-Self Patriotic Move-ment (TSPM). The journal *Tian Feng* explained:

> The goal of self-propagation is not the unification or modification of belief, but the thoroughgoing eradication of vestiges of imperialist thought, and the bringing of preaching into harmony with the true gospel of Jesus Christ. We should have mutual respect for differences that exist among the churches in creed, organization and ritual.[38]

It is important to note that, in spite of these reassurances, union still required acceptance of the state's agenda in terms of ideological remolding and monitoring. In order to accomplish this, the 1954 con-ference established three *political* points of Protestant unity: the erad-ication of imperialist thought in the churches, acceptance of Protes-tant union based on the "common ground" of patriotic support of the government, and the establishment of the principle of mutual respect of theological differences.

Wang Mingdao and the United Front

By 1953, the CCP had imprisoned most indigenous Protestant church leaders and had broken up their churches. Wang Mingdao, however, remained free and continued to hold services. His friendships with Christian pastors and congregations throughout the nation, his high esteem amongst Christians generally, and his national and international reputation as well as the wide distribution of his journal *Spiritual Food Quarterly* made him difficult to remove without creating a ruckus. This was especially true up until 1954, when Three-Self leaders were trying to coax reluctant conservatives into the movement.

Meanwhile, in the World Council of Churches there were sharp disagreements as to how to respond to events in China. Some defended the Three-Self Reform Movement and supported their moves to cut off foreign ties and to consolidate the church. Others, however, believed that the Communist Party was attempting to quash Christianity in China through its manipulation of the Three-Self Reform Movement. Both sides, however, watched Wang Mingdao's situation closely in order to discern how the new government would deal with Christian dissent. Rumors that Wang had been arrested and perhaps even executed created a stir at the 1954 World Council of Churches conference in Geneva.[39] Although the rumors were false, their very existence demonstrated that any untoward treatment of Wang Mingdao could cause difficulties at a time when the Communist Party was beginning to reestablish international relationships.

For his part, Wang kept a low profile by avoiding open conflict with the state. His desire was simply to maintain his independence from any union that would affect his church. At the same time, Wang Mingdao resisted all attempts to get him to join the Three-Self Reform Movement. Wang had no desire to defy state authority in political matters, but he was convinced that joining the movement was a religious matter and thus protected under the constitution. Prior to 1954, Wang's dissent was allowed to stand. After 1954, with union secured, the CCP determined that Wang's resistance was a liability they would no longer tolerate.

FOUR

Strange News

The Nation As Gospel

The war of words that erupted between Wang Mingdao and the leaders of the Three-Self Movement quickly became part of the larger ideological campaigns that swept over China in 1954. The campaign to discover and purge the nation's enemies, hiding under the cloak of respectability, began with a campaign against a wayward intellectual named Hu Feng. Although Hu Feng had supported Mao and the Communist Party before and after the revolution, like his protégé the noted writer and social critic Lu Xun, Hu reserved the right to chide the Party when he found their cultural and literary dictates stifling. Hu railed against Party hacks ensconced by the government to champion revolutionary literature in New China. The servile drivel they served up only "suffocates life," he opined.[1] He depicted the literary bureaucrats that opposed his views as a "dictatorial clique who treated all who disagreed with them as enemies." It had become so bad, Hu complained, that "the people cannot even fart disapproval."[2]

Championing "diversity and creativity in China's cultural life," Hu Feng attempted a literary putsch. He attacked in print the cultural and literary status quo of the Communist Party. This putsch, however, came to a swift end when some of Hu's protégés dared to ridicule the works of Mao himself. Led by Mao, the reaction of the government was swift and severe.[3] Hu Feng was first denounced in the press, then detained by the Security Bureau and finally forced to confess his counterrevolutionary crimes at a public tribunal. A broken man, he committed suicide not long after his imprisonment.

The death of Hu Feng, however, did not end matters. By May 1955 a nationwide Anti-Hu Feng campaign was launched to "liquidate all Hu Feng elements throughout the country." The Party warned that Hu Feng elements were everywhere. Hidden "beneath the cloak of respectable vocations," these "enemies of the people" were bent on subverting the revolution and the nation.[4] Primarily, these Hu Feng elements were intellectuals and others who had earlier dared to air grievances with the state or resist ideological indoctrination. Accordingly, if the nation were to progress and prosper, these Hu Feng elements had to be ferreted out and liquidated.[5]

That Wang Mingdao was caught up in the dragnet of this campaign reveals much about the threat he represented. Certainly, the contrast between Wang Mingdao and Hu Feng could hardly be more striking. Wang was a conservative Christian evangelist and pastor, while Hu was an intellectual atheist. Wang spent his life working in the church, Hu worked in the academy. What is important, however, is what they had in common. Each in their own way tore at the rhetorical and institutional glue that justified Communist Party control over all aspects of life. Hu Feng desired merely to free literature from the straitjacket of the political line. Wang Mingdao wished nothing more than for his church to serve God and to be a witness to fallen society. Yet, it was these very sentiments that brought them between the cross hairs of the Communist Party. Hu Feng sought to free literature from the confines of suffocating political ideology; Wang Mingdao worked to liberate the church and its doctrine from the same. These stands fundamentally challenged the right of the government to determine the true nature of human existence.

Neither believed that his views represented any real threat to the government. This would prove a devastating miscalculation for both.

What Hu Feng failed to realize, and Wang Mingdao realized only partially, was that by refusing to allow the ideology of the state to define the identity and the nature of existence in China, they represented a threat that would not be tolerated.

Initial Skirmishes

Up to 1954, steady pressure was put on Wang Mingdao to join the conference in Beijing to officially recognize the Three-Self Patriotic Movement (TSPM). He was warned that failure to do so would have dire consequences. As the conference neared, several senior church officials arrived at his front door hoping to pressure Wang to join, but he remained in his room and refused to meet or speak with them. A few days later a circular was distributed to all churches and Christian organizations in Beijing to appoint representatives to attend a public denunciation of Wang Mingdao.[6]

A month after the conference, public security officers arrived at Wang's home and escorted him to a hall filled with Christians and Three-Self leaders. He was taken up to the stage and turned toward the crowd. Those designated to bring charges against him angrily accused him of being a reactionary, a counterrevolutionary, and a vile enemy of the people. As these charges were leveled against him, Wang stood impassively on the stage, "his eyes fixed on the ceiling never uttering a word."[7] The plan of a typical accusation meeting was to whip the crowd into a frenzy so that they would demand harsh sentences against the accused. With Wang Mingdao standing before them, however, the crowd "sat silent," and some even wept openly. After the meeting fizzled, Wang was returned home to ponder his response.[8]

Sensing that things were going Wang's way, Christian students sympathetic to Wang began an "Oppose the Persecution of Wang Mingdao Campaign."[9] Prior to his public denunciation, Wang's resistance toward the Three-Self Movement had been passive. He had advised the members of his church simply to avoid political campaigns and denunciations when possible and to resist indoctrination through disciplined silence. Both in his writing and from the pulpit, he had studiously avoided any direct reference to the Three-Self Movement or the political situation in China. The denunciation changed all that, however. His confidence bolstered, Wang unleashed his pen against the Three-Self Movement and its leaders.

This began with a series of carefully crafted commentaries on Scripture printed in his journal *Spiritual Food Quarterly*. The article "Obey God or Obey Men?" commented on the Apostles who preached the Gospel and were persecuted by "Religious Leaders" who tried to stop them. The Apostles were not deterred, in Wang's words, by the "thundering madness and power" of the "political and religious leaders." Instead,

> ... because of the courageous and firm stand of the apostles, the gospel was nevertheless spread abroad and the Church established. The believers who followed also took courage and stood their ground, spreading the gospel all over the world.

Drawing the lines together, Wang challenged Christians to follow the example of the Apostles and not those of religious leaders.

> Some have asked me what path the Church should take today. I answer: unquestionably, the path of the apostles. That is, follow the apostles by imitating their courageous and firm stand, not being afraid of any *threats*, not holding life dear being faithful unto death, not pleasing men. . . .

Wang then turns the screw assailing craven and corrupt leaders that debase the Church by submitting it to human authority.

> It is lamentable that many Christian leaders use the principle of obedience to man's rules and submission to man's authority to cover up their cowardice and failure. They thus deceive many believers who don't fully understand the truths of the Bible. This results in the faith of the Church and the ministry being subordinated to the rule of men and men's authority. The truth then becomes obscured, the Bible misinterpreted, the foundations of the Church undermined and the flock scattered. The Church and the gospel of Christ are thereby degraded

and put on a lower plane than compliance to men's rules and submitting to human authority. These foundations and precious things are so lightly surrendered by some so-called servants of God! How can such Christian leaders then escape the wrath of God?[10]

It was not difficult for Wang's audience to read between the lines, and they knew to whom he referred. Wang's charge was that because the TSPM had been conceived in fear, its bitter fruit was idolatry, with deference to those in power displacing true reverence and worship of God.

Although biting, such criticism was cleverly indirect. When Three-Self leaders responded virulently in print that the "religious leaders" Wang criticized in Scripture were actually veiled references to themselves, they found themselves not only criticized by Wang but condemned by Scripture as well.

In his commentary "The Missing Voice" Wang lifted up Micaiah, the true prophet of Israel who resisted the four hundred false prophets flattering wicked King Ahab even as they led Israel astray. From this Wang observed that the true prophet stands alone and is opposed by the many and the powerful. The true prophet speaks the word of God regardless of consequences, while false prophets measure their words to indulge the king with flattery and assurance of good fortune in order to gain favor.[11] Authoritative and direct, the true prophet's words sting with the admonishment of hard truth. Obsequious and diversionary, the words of the false prophets comfit the king even when disaster is imminent. Even though genuine prophets are few, they are those that speak the truth and because they do they are mistreated by those in power. As Wang explained:

Such people are so rare in the world. Such people are even rarer in the Church. They are scarce among believers and scarcer still among Christian leaders. There were four hundred prophets who flattered Ahab but only one prophet who did not value his own welfare, who did not care that others slandered him, because he was determined simply to be faithful to God. The situation in the nation of Israel in those days is parallel to that in the Church of God today. The faithful prophets of God are hated and persecuted wherever they are. But there are two kinds of people who hate and persecute them the most. There are those who are being rebuked and warned but who refuse to repent. And there are those who are unfaithful in preaching God's Word but who habitually flatter and praise men.[12]

Again, Wang's allusion was clear. The leaders of the TSPM had bent low at the altar of political power and now were opposed to him because he spoke the truth. Like the four hundred false prophets, they sought to silence the truth of God by silencing his prophet. Thus Wang wrote in another article:

Today the Church is in a sad state, burning incense to all kinds of "golden calves" and worshipping at strange altars. Many preachers who should be rebuking sin with God's Word have become silent. Among them, some are afraid to risk danger and calamity, and so they dare not open their mouths for God. Others are out for their own bene-fit, which requires that they please men. Therefore they cannot speak the truth of God. . . . At this time what the Church urgently needs are prophets who are not afraid of power people.[13]

This figurative use of characters from the Bible was not just a strategic ploy. Wang used biblical characters and narratives to frame and discern the true import of events unfolding around him. From the stories of Nebuchadnezzar and Daniel to the apostles and the religious leaders, Wang turned to the biblical narrative to make sense of his resistance to the religious status quo. Thus, the truth of Scripture was to be found not simply in ideas abstracted from the text, but in the stories themselves, which provided the interpretive lens by which to make sense of the surrounding events. Though the names might have changed, the fundamental conflict between faith and unbelief remained the same.

This was hardly escapist. By turning to the biblical narrative, he offered a significantly different version of what was taking place. Accordingly, Wang renarrated the events that engulfed him in light of biblical stories, which unveiled their true significance. This was Wang at his prophetic best as he cast current events in their true bib-lical light. When events were seen in their true perspective, this allowed wise Christians to take on their proper role in the unfolding drama swirling around them. Only then could their faithfulness or unfaithfulness be fitly manifested, understood, and measured. Accordingly, Christian faith could never be reduced to mere personal opinion or private sentiment, consolation or comfort, or refuge from the harsh realities of life. No, Christian faith was something real and prophetic; it brought to light the true essence of the human drama now taking shape before their eyes.

More immediately, Wang's exegesis unmasked the true essence of his accusers: false prophets ensnared in ideological idolatry that corrupted the church. Thus, he threatened both the appointed leadership of the TSPM and the rhetoric of CCP ideology. Unlike Y. T. Wu, Wang did not see the divine in the revolution and its rhetoric, but rather ancient heresies disguised in new robes that continued to imperil God's people.

The Necessity of Suffering

Wang's commentaries also emphasized the necessity of persecution and suffering for all those who would resist idolatry and evil. Suffering, however, was not a sign of defeat and dishonor but rather a badge of honor and a powerful weapon against the enemies of God's elect. Suffering revealed the ultimate struggle between God's sovereign rule and the disorder of rebellious humankind. The weapons waged against God's people were temptation, threat, and persecution. The enemies' plan was to corrupt Christians' witness through temptation or fear. Truth, holiness, and suffering were the weapons of the church to overcome evil. If truth exposed evil, holiness kept it at bay, but it was suffering that in the end vanquished evil.

Thus persecution and suffering were redemptive and always preceded purification, vindication, and the expansion of the church through history. So certain was Wang that persecution actually served God's ends that he was confident that the threats leveled against him would not be carried through. His successful resistance to the Japanese and the failure of his antagonists to successfully render charges against him at his public denunciation led him to conclude that his enemies saw the ultimate futility of persecution.

> Though there might be ways to suppress Christians and keep them from preaching Christ, the leaders figured that the safest and easiest way was simply to threaten. If they used more drastic measures, it might bring the matter to public attention and cause a bad reaction. Another great concern to them was that the more they persecuted the sincere Christians, the stronger they might become in their faith. To use drastic measures against them would be equal to encouraging the progress of their faith. Having such concern, those that were more far-sighted and more thoughtful would not advocate harsh ways to oppose the gospel, but relied on threatening.[14]

Thus, the key to the unfolding drama was for the church and its spokespersons not to succumb to threat but to continue to preach the Gospel and to spread the faith. Wang explained:

> wherever the gospel of Christ is preached it meets opposition: at the same time there are always people accepting it, whatever the consequences and becoming Christians. The greatest hope of those who opposed Christ was that believers would rebel against Christ and believe in him no longer. But, should this hope fail, at least they might retreat for a while and stop preaching Christ. In that way, no more people would turn to Christ. And when Christians stopped increasing, the gospel of Christ would gradually die out of its own accord.[15]

In short, just as Christ suffered at the hands of the government and the religious officials of his day, so now the spectacle was being replayed by those who refused to join the TSPM. Those who attacked faithful Christians were one with those who had crucified Christ. Those who refused to suffer and denied Christ were one with Judas, while those willing to suffer were one with Christ and the apostles.

Of all the biblical figures Wang alluded to, none was as important as the apostle Peter. At first, Peter was not prepared to suffer and so denied Christ. Later, however, confronted with the risen Christ, Peter came to "fully comprehend that the only way to overcome the enemy's threat and attacks" was to "arm himself with the spirit of suffering."

Only with this spirit, according to Wang, could fear be overcome. Only then could a Christian be invincible and "continuously victorious." As Wang explained:

> Previously he [Peter] had been afraid of suffering, so he had lied and denied his Lord in order to escape the suffering—and had fallen into lamentable failure. But now he was ready to suffer; he did not try to avoid danger. So the enemy could no longer overcome him. He had continual victories. He had deeply apprehended this truth through his own experience; therefore he could encourage the Church, saying, "Therefore, since Christ has suffered in the flesh, arm yourselves also with the same purpose."[16]

This passage about Peter foreshadowed the events that would mark Wang's own arrest, imprisonment, and subsequent confession. Like Peter, Wang's fear of suffering led to his being broken in prison, where he was forced to confess his crimes and to publicly denounce his former stand against the TSPM. Just like Peter, however, Wang eventually overcame his fear and failure and willingly embraced his own suffering by repudiating his confession.

Figuratively Deconstructing the TSPM

As we have seen, Wang's commentaries allowed him to defend his own position and to undermine, albeit indirectly, that of his accusers. More important, by transposing the political rhetoric aimed against him into a biblical key, he turned their indictments back upon them. When his opponents complained that they were the scribes, religious officials, and false prophets Wang was maligning, he could simply muse upon how they came to recognize themselves.

Wang's arguments were more than a gambit, since they drew their symbolic and narrative power from Scripture. The "suffering servant of God" and "the true prophet of Israel" challenged the rhetoric of the Communist Party and the TSPM and found it wanting. This was a war to decide whose rhetoric, drama, and sacred text would define the church in China: the ideology of the state or the dramatic narrative of the Bible.

The Response of the TSPM

Wang's commentaries hit their mark. Wounded by his innuendo, the official publications of the TSPM struck back. K. H. Ting wrote:

> In recent years, Wang Mingdao has published many articles, most of them expressing his hatred toward New China and his irrational thinking. He has told us that the Christian's view of life should be different from that of unbelievers. He has tried to develop hatred among the Chinese Christians toward New China and has compared China with the kingdom of Nebuchanezzar and Christians with Daniel and his three associates. However, he mentions nothing of imperialism or of using religion to control people. On the contrary, he states that "the imperialism you mention is just the truth of the Bible." He does everything to misconstrue our self-governing, self-propagating, and self-supporting principles and has distorted people's understanding of the Three-Self Movement, even accusing its leaders of being false prophets and disciples of Judas.[17]

According to this perspective, Wang's ambivalence to imperialism was evidence of his reactionary roots and his use of the Bible and biblical figures a mere feint to hide his political motivation.

> Wang Mingdao is a talented speaker, and some argue that he simply explains the Bible clearly and logically. In truth, his use of the Bible is purely politically motivated. Before the revolution he wrote that servants should obey their masters attentively and fearfully, that their obedience reflected their obedience to God. After the revolution he changed his tune. He says now that fearing humans and seeking their approval manifests unbelief. In this we can discern his true thoughts. Look at how he changes the view of the Bible to suit his need. Is his faith really exemplary? Are his character and motives pure?[18]

Whereas Wang revealed what he regarded as the true nature of his accusers through biblical figures, the TSPM's rejoinder sought to uncover the true political essence of Wang Mingdao. Beneath Wang's biblical allusions, they argued, lay a reactionary core that had to be exposed. Thus one TSPM apologist wrote:

> The whole truth about Wang Mingdao has been uncovered, and we must draw a line between the people and counterrevolutionaries. It has nothing to do with religion. Counterrevolution is one matter, religion is another. We are not to confuse them. It is our duty to strip away the religious cloak of Wang Mingdao and thoroughly to expose his counterrevolutionary essence.[19]

Certainly several avenues were open to Wang's opponents. Wang's interpretations of Scripture could have been challenged on a variety of biblical or theological grounds, yet his opponents did not strike here. Rather, they focused on Wang's "counterrevolutionary" character. In short, Communist political ideology provided the foundation and rhetoric in their case against Wang Mingdao. If one assumes, as Wang's opponents did, that political essence is the ground of human existence, then profession, religion, clan affiliation, and the like are mere cloaks veiling an individual's true essence. The fact that Wang Mingdao preached from the Bible and argued accordingly only masked his true identity. His religious views, his character, his virtues, and his vices, they argued, could be fully understood only according to the deep structure of political ideology.

As their arguments reveal, Wang's detractors held that political essence not only precedes religious essence; it defines it. Thus, duty to the nation defines duty to God making Wang's refusal to unite with the TSPM a betrayal not only of country, but of Christ and the church. K. H. Ting explained:

> Because of his [Wang Mingdao's] hatred toward the church, toward the Three-Self Movement and its leaders, he insists on dividing the church. Either as a Chinese who loves the nation or as a Christian who loves the church, he must realize the importance of unity. . . . The Three-Self Movement seeks to unify all believers together to be against imperialism and to love the nation. There is no excuse for a

believer not to join the movement—unless one does not want to be against imperialism.[20]

Wang's refusal to join the TSPM was a crime not because it threatened church unity but precisely because it threatened *national* unity and identity. Wang's judgment of the TSPM was, in fact, a judgment on the nation, and his call for a public presence of the church apart from the TSPM was counterrevolutionary because he sought to divide that which had now become one in essence. Once one accepts the narrative of the nation-state as the common ground of unity, rationality, and human identity, challenging that unity at any level is by nature counterrevolutionary.

Thus, in their opening salvo the TSPM sought to turn the tables on Wang Mingdao by changing the story. What Wang had portrayed as a biblical and theological conflict, the TSPM framed as a political conflict. By attacking the TSPM, Wang had struck at the ideology of the state and was thus being isolated and identified as an enemy of the CCP.

"Truth or Poison?"

The battle joined, Wang Mingdao swiftly countered with two essays that directly challenged the TSPM and its leadership. The first, "Truth or Poison?" undermined the TSPM's attempt to purge Christianity in China of the Western imperialism that they argued had poisoned the minds of Chinese Christians. Wang wrote:

> They say, "imperialism has poisoned our thinking and covered up the true light of the gospel . . . [and] God is calling today's Chinese church to a special task to purge 'imperialist poisonous thought' and to spread the pure gospel."[21]

What is "imperialist poisonous thought," Wang queried, and what part of the Christian missionary message needed to be purged? Wang argued that these questions needed to be addressed, because the TSPM's lack of specificity had led to anxiety and fear in the church. He explained:

Many preachers, though they know they should preach the truth of the Bible, are afraid that others will accuse them of spreading imperialist poisonous thought, so they quiver in fear and avoid opening themselves to attack in their preaching. The result is that their preaching comes to nothing: no content and no power.[22]

In spite of the need for clarification, none was forthcoming from the TSPM leaders. Wang charged that such evasion was by design. The goal of the TSPM leaders was to manipulate and control pastors and church leaders through fear. In Wang's words, "They do not explain what imperialist poisonous thought is even as Christians vainly pursue its meaning. They equivocate for they are sly. They conceal their true face so as to leave believers vainly stumbling in the dark."[23] Nonetheless, what Wang held the TSPM officials knew in secret, he was ready to proclaim outright, that the campaign against "imperialist poisonous thought" was in fact an attack on the gospel itself. Thus, in "Truth or Poison?" Wang sought to expose the ideological foundations that put the TSPM directly at odds with the gospel.

According to the TSPM, they were simply trying to unify Christians in support of the country. What hindered this work was the "imperialist poison [that separated] believers from the masses." Thus, the TSPM leaders argued that reactionary distinctions between believers and unbelievers rent asunder the solidarity Christians should have with the masses in order to establish the united front. The TSPM's subsequent campaign to remove "imperialist poison" from the consciousness of believers was meant to eliminate the harmful division between church and society, believers and unbelievers, the saved and unsaved.[24]

The problem with this campaign, according to Wang, was that the distinction it sought to remove was biblical. Without this necessary distinction between believers and unbelievers as well as the church and the world, the gospel was unintelligible. Wang turned to Scripture and cited a host of biblical texts that made no sense apart from their being a necessary biblical distinction between believers and unbelievers. He then challenged his opponents to either refute the meaning of these passages or conclude that what they called "imperialist poison" was in fact the gospel.[25]

Let me ask if what I have written here is a distortion of the Bible? I have argued only upon the testimony of Scripture. The words are not many or difficult to understand, nor do they require in-depth analysis. Anyone with true faith in the Lord can understand what I have written. I simply ask whether these passages from Scripture are imperialist poisonous thought? If not, please inform those you have trapped in fear. If they are, then kindly remove your own mask and state . . . that you are not Christians and that you are not true leaders of the church. If you argue that Christ and his teachings are in error, you are truly an "anti-Christian institution" and a new "anti-Christian movement." At least then you would be honest.[26]

As before, the simplicity of Wang's argument belies its cleverness. Prior to 1949, Y. T. Wu or T. C. Chao simply would have dismissed Wang's separation of believers and unbelievers as escapist and biblicist. After 1949, however, such a rejoinder would jeopardize the tenuous union forged between liberals and evangelicals within the TSPM. Conservatives forced to choose between Wang's evangelical distinction between believers and unbelievers and the universalism of Wu and Chao would side with Wang. This, in turn, would unravel the slender cords holding together the TSPM.

Though clever tactically, the true import of Wang's argument was to assail the theological implications of union in the TSPM. He realized that many evangelicals had joined the TSPM in the naïve belief that union meant only patriotic support of the nation. In fact, Wang argued, union required that they sunder Christianity from Scripture, sound doctrine, and the essence and mission of the church. Without the distinction between believers and unbelievers, biblical terms such as *sin, repentance, conversion,* and *sanctification* had vanished into the political rhetoric of united front ideology. As a result, the state-sanctioned churches had become ornamental shells whose true essence had been "aborted." Thus Wang wrote:

> Those people opposed to God do not fear a church that is merely formal and in name only but with no essential faith. That church in the world has neither influence nor power. That church is not able to bring life or power to anyone, neither does it bother anyone; nonetheless, it does provide color and festivities, and it is lovely to

look at. Those opposed to God do not hate this kind of church, and they wish to convert the church to this form, which, though it has its worship hall and ceremony, in fact represents the destruction of the church.[27]

In conclusion, Wang gave a stern warning to Christians to resist the TSPM's coercion and corruption. If they were persecuted it would only stiffen resistance, spread the gospel, and in the end strengthen the church and expose the lie being foisted upon them by "false prophets" and "disciples of Judas."

Antagonistic Contradictions: The TSPM Responds

This direct broadside upon the ethos of the TSPM did not go unanswered. An article soon appeared in the *Nanjing Theological Review* that was then distributed to church officials and workers across China to be read and adopted as the official stand of the TSPM and the Religious Affairs Bureau (RAB) against Wang Mingdao. The article was written under a pen name, but the author's familiarity with the work of Nietzsche and Reinhold Niebuhr as well as the important status given to the article suggests that Y. T. Wu penned it. As head of the TSPM and given the fragility of the TSPM union, it makes sense that Wu would use a pen name so as to maintain his status as an impartial arbiter above the fray,

The essay, entitled "Biblical Truth and Imperialist Poisonous Thought Are Absolutely Incompatible," sought to uncover the true issues at stake between Wang Mingdao and the TSPM and in so doing to expose the true motive behind Wang's dissidence.[28] In a pattern that would repeat itself throughout the conflict, Wang's antagonist studiously avoids Wang's biblical argument. Rather, he turns to the larger political contours that would allow readers to discern the true essence of the conflict. According to the article, two monumental historical forces have defined the modern era: imperialism and revolution. Locked in a bitter struggle, these forces now contended for the heart and soul of the church. On one side were those in the TSPM, who had joined the masses to support the revolution. On the other side were reactionaries such as Wang Mingdao who defended the forces of imperialism and fomented counterrevolutionary reaction.

The author argues that the TSPM's position is theologically sound because God is not just God of the Jews but of all people. Thus, a proper understanding of God's love must take into account the just struggle of the masses. It was this just struggle that the TSPM had taken up in its campaign against "imperialist poison." In contrast to the TSPM's common cause with the struggle of the masses, Wang Mingdao had focused on minor distinctions between Christians and the masses. Thus, rather than opposing imperialism, Wang chose to breed hatred for the masses and their just revolution. This revealed Wang's imperialist designs cloaked in religious language.[29] Thus, the author notes:

> Imperialists use all their methods to destroy our unity. They exaggerate small issues that really should not effect unity, while at the same time they ignore the big issue of the anti-imperialist struggle. They sow discord and spread slanderous rumors. In doing so they invert the order of importance of the issues at stake. This is just the tactic of this man who has led the fight against the Three-Self Patriotic Movement.[30]

Turning up the heat, Wang's antagonist claimed this dissent wasn't merely a theological error but inferred that Wang had committed a political crime. He explained:

> Even as the masses have allowed the church to worship God under the guidance of the Three-Self Patriotic Movement, so we must be vigilant to prevent imperialists from sowing discord among us *by their agents.* These spread discontent with the Three-Self Patriotic Movement to destroy unity and obscure *the distinction between the enemy and us.* We must unite to strengthen anti-imperialist and patriotic power. In seeking common ground while respecting differences, we preserve unity and strike a heavy blow against imperialism.[31]

Attacking the ideology of the state made one an enemy of the state and subject to its authority. Wang knew this as well as anyone, the writer argued, so Wang appealed to Scripture and doctrine. Nevertheless, his appeals were nothing more than a ruse to hide his true counterrevolutionary identity "under the cloak of religion."

> To destroy the Three-Self Patriotic Movement, they had to try to create a scandal over belief, so that Christians cannot unite. As everybody knew when we started down the path of the Three-Self Patriotic Movement, we would never let our faith degenerate, but what could degenerate was our political stand. Imperialists did not like this. Thus, Wang Mingdao and his colleagues had to shout their abuse and hate us to the very marrow of their bones.[32]

This stinging attack was followed by a series of harsh editorials attacking Wang. In the summer of 1955, even the national newspaper *Remin Ribao* chimed in, charging that Wang was a Hu Feng element. A fresh denunciation campaign against Wang Mingdao was ordered in churches across the nation, and on July 31 Wang's crimes against the nation were listed in *Tian Feng*.

"We Because of Faith"

Wang, however, did not back down. Convinced that this was a spiritual and religious conflict and that the government would respect his freedom of belief, he drafted his last and perhaps his most important written work: "We Because of Faith." In "Truth or Poison?" Wang took issue with the rhetoric of the TSPM. In "We Because of Faith" he took on the institution itself.

Wang began "We Because of Faith" with his basic thesis that his conflict with the TSPM was theological not political. To prove his claim, Wang noted that the divide between him and the leadership of the TSPM was over twenty years old and had always concerned doctrinal issues such as biblical authority, miracles, the atonement, and the second coming of Christ. As Y. T. Wu himself had argued before the revolution, between modernists and fundamentalists there could be no union. In this earlier sentiment of Wu, Wang was in full agreement because, he argued, Christianity represented more than a name one chose, it was a faith in Christ and an adherence to what

Scripture revealed about him. To suggest otherwise consigned Scripture and doctrine to irrelevancy.

That modernists were now agreeable to union with evangelicals for political sake did not surprise Wang. Modernists viewed Scripture as mere symbol and myth, so doctrine was endlessly malleable to meet the need of the day. This luxury was impossible for those like Wang who held that Scripture was the inspired Word of God and the doctrine that flowed from it authoritative. For Wang, evangelical faith demanded that Scripture order the faith, life, and union of the church, not political expediency. Thus, Wang resisted union with the TSPM, for in the end it forced him to unite with those who denied the essentials of Christian faith.[33]

This did not mean it was impermissible for Christians to join in common cause with non-Christians. What Wang objected to was not common cause on issues that affected both Christian and non-Christian alike. Wang objected to the demand of the TSPM that Christians like himself ignore heresy in their own ranks by entering into Christian union with those who deny Christianity's central tenets. "For such people, there cannot be talk about respect or union. These people have no faith; they do not believe in Jesus; they are not Christians." Because they represented alternative faiths, Wang argued that the chasm between fundamentalists and modernists could not be bridged without making a mockery of what Christians professed to believe in.[34]

Wang then replied to K. H. Ting, the former Anglican and future head of the TSPM who had argued against Wang that Christian unity did not require doctrinal unity with regard to Jesus Christ. Ting argued that, because all Christians believed "in the same Heavenly Father and the same Bible .·. . are redeemed by the same Christ [and] are guided by the same Holy Spirit," they did not need to agree on specific matters that had traditionally divided modernists and fundamentalists.[35] In Wang's estimation, Ting's logic was monistic and not trinitarian:

The modernists who explain away the fundamental doctrines about Christ and say they are not essential to faith, are they not dishonoring, despising, and denying the Son? Are they not "transgressing, and abiding not in the doctrine of Christ?" If they treat Christ thus, then how are they treating the Father? To say one believes in the Father is not enough; he must also believe in the Son as proof that he believes in the Father. Since the modernists do not honor the Son, since they despise Him and deny Him, since they transgress and abide not in His doctrine, how can we acknowledge that they believe with us in the same Father?[36]

Wang's demand that the Father can only be known through the Son and the Son only through a proper understanding of Scripture in accord with sound doctrine illuminated the theological divide in interesting ways. The demand that Jesus Christ and sound doctrine defined the nature of the church created problems for those who sought to establish the church on secular philosophical, social, or political foundations. The appeal of Ting's amorphous First Person of the Trinity lay in the fact that it gave tremendous freedom to fashion Christianity according to a secular ideological framework. Wang's emphasis that the Father could only be fully known through the Son, not through creation, sundered that union. This made the church, theology, and doctrine far less malleable.

Moreover, Wang protested that his distinction between believers from unbelievers was not "condemning men before God . . . reviling them and praying to God not to save them," as had been suggested in rebuttals to his "Truth or Poison?" He explained that the label "unbelievers is not a label we put on people. It is a description of a certain kind of people who do not believe the truths of the Bible that must be accepted by faith."[37] In spite of the possibility of misunderstanding and misrepresentation, Wang argued, such a distinction must be preserved in order to retain the nature and mission of the church.

Wang further stated that the theological distinctions between modernists and fundamentalists, as well as believers and unbelievers, were clear and easy for all to see. The fact that his opponents used manipulation, coercion, and threat to force him and other Christians to deny this truth only revealed his opponents' true nature. Thus he wrote:

Indisputable facts which have existed for scores of years and still stand clearly before our eyes—how can they be wiped out by a few artificial and empty slogans? Christians with any faith and common sense will see what they are up to. We all remember the story of the Jewish leaders accusing Jesus before Pilate. But Jesus was not the injured party; His accusers injured themselves. They sent Jesus into glory while they themselves encountered the wrath of God.

Although others might have succumbed to such tactics, Wang would not. He insisted on the independence and autonomy of the church as the essence of true Christianity.

> A final word, in all seriousness. We will not unite in any way with these unbelievers, nor will we join any of their organizations. And even with true believers we can only enjoy a spiritual union. There should not be any kind of formal, organizational union, because we cannot find any teaching in the Bible to support it. Our attitude in matters of faith is this: all truths that are found in the Bible we accept and hold. Whatever teachings are not in the Bible we totally reject. For our loyalty to God we are ready to pay any cost that is required. We shall shrink from no sacrifice. Misrepresentation and slander can never intimidate us. Everyone has a mouth with which he can say what he pleases. But facts are facts forever. God sees them clearly and God's people see them clearly, no matter how others may twist them or malign us. We take our stand on Christian doctrine. We because of faith![38]

Changing the Subject

At the heart of this war of words between Wang and the TSPM lay two significantly different perceptions of the conflict based on radically different historical and narrative planes. For Wang Mingdao, the conflict was but an age-old struggle prefigured in Scripture and now being played out between the faithful and their modernist antagonists. The players might have changed, but the drama remained the same. The task of the church was to remain faithful to preach the gospel in a hostile world. Its enemies were religious and political officials bent on silencing their rival, the church, to prevent the spread of the gospel. In the view of the TSPM, the conflict was defined according to the ideology of the revolution, the good news revealed in political and ideological idiom. The vanguard of this gospel was not the church but the revolution. Thus, the goal of the TSPM was to enlighten Christians, who had been previously blind to the truth, that they might recognize and involve themselves in God's revolutionary action in the world. Those foolish enough to stand in the way of this divine tide deserved to be swept away by the progressive forces of history.

Had this been a mere clash of differing visions of the church, it might easily be dismissed as a minor eddy in the greater struggle between Protestant liberalism and fundamentalism. Behind the rhetoric, however, a silent power observed and directed the forces at play. Even if Wang won points against his sparring partners in the TSPM, he badly miscalculated the nature, power, and concerns of those who wielded real political power. These were powerful officials who believed that their dominion was not secure until all life conformed to their political ideology.

Both submission and resistance to political ideology had their cost. Resistance meant arrest and imprisonment for Wang Mingdao, but there were costs for those who had joined the TSPM as well. T. C. Chao and Y. T. Wu believed that in the establishment of the People's Republic the great ends of the Social Gospel would be realized. With the arrival of the "new society," however, the need for a Social Gospel vanished. They learned too late that when social righteousness is politically established, Christianity and the church are of no use to the political powers. This was certainly the expectation of the Communist Party, which believed that religion would diminish in the face of the dialectical progress of history and society. Nonetheless, for Modernists such as Y. T. Wu now charged with leading and preserving the church, social and political progress presented a painful crisis when they finally recognized that they stood at the helm of an irrelevant institution. By 1958, those Christians who had drunk deeply from the spring of Marxist ideology now saw in their present situation the death of Christianity. To console them, Y. T. Wu wrote the following:

But new questions, of a more basic nature, are now coming up. . . .
Marxism-Leninism, they say is the leading ideology in China and is

being taught in schools and colleges. Under its impact, what will become of the young people—or even older ones who are already believers? And what chances will there be of making new converts? It is true that this constitutes a deep-seated contradiction. But if we look it in the face its seemingly ominous character disappears. My answer is this: Let the Christian Faith prove itself. If it is such a fragile thing that it cannot stand up in a critical philosophical environment, its death should be a matter of regret to nobody. But if it is a staunch, virile, life-giving faith that every devout Christian believes it to be, its vital testimony will always convince people because it meets the spiritual needs and eternal yearnings of the human heart.[39]

Although this statement captures well the pathos felt by Christians in the TSPM, what strikes one as strange is Wu's view that a "staunch, virile, life-giving faith" could now only meet "spiritual needs and eternal yearnings." Only a decade before he would have dismissed such escapist sentimentalism as a form of superstition whose time was past.

However, such was the unavoidable conclusion to Wu's "socialist religion." In the end, the state's religious character effaced the need of the church. Once the progressive state replaced God, the closing of sixty-one out of sixty-five churches in Beijing and the reduction of the number of churches in Shanghai from over two hundred to only twenty-three made perfect sense. Likewise, it seemed only logical for pastors to cease their "meaningless gesticulations" in sanctuaries on Sundays and to engage in the true worship of harvesting real grain in real fields or working in factories so that the production quotas of the state might be met. Thus by 1958, it only seemed right to work on Sundays in order to increase state agricultural output and joyfully to turn over church properties to the state as "an expression of Chinese Christians' long cherished hope for unity and a contribution to the nation as represented by the more economical use of resources."[40]

These events bring to light the paradoxical reversal of positions of the antagonists in this debate. Those who sought social and political relevance through the Social Gospel in fact guided the church to its vanishing point. What was left was a shell devoid of relevance, save only to meet the "spiritual needs and eternal yearnings of the human heart." On the other hand, Wang Mingdao found himself at the center of attention as one who had vexed the political and religious authorities enough to demand the arrest and imprisonment of a fifty-six-year-old pacifist pastor.

FIVE

Dividing the Nation

The Arrest and Confession of Wang Mingdao

I am a counter-revolutionary offender. As a result of the patient attitude shown by the Government and the re-education given me I have
come to realize my errors. I have been accorded generous treatment
by the Government and have been saved from the abyss of crime. For
this my heart is full of gratitude. When I think of what I did in the
past I am deeply distressed and ashamed. Already I have made a frank
statement of my offenses to the Government. Today I simply want to
talk to you about how I used religious forms to carry on counterrevolutionary activities.

Wang Mingdao (1956)[1]

By August 1955, the noose was beginning to tighten on Wang
Mingdao. Throughout the spring and summer a steady drum-
beat of editorials in the religious and secular press vilified Wang
Mingdao's errant political stance. In July, *Tian Feng* published a list
of Wang's "crimes" and called for swift punishment. Members of his
church were ordered to attend denunciation meetings and pressured
to expose the crimes of Wang Mingdao. Others noticed that they

were being followed on their way to church, and Wang's neighbors observed strangers peering over the wall of the parsonage as though looking for ways to enter.[2]

Wang Mingdao sensed trouble closing in but was unsure as to what end. Wang's sermon August 7, "This Is How They Betrayed the Son of Man," reflected his angst as some seven hundred to eight hundred worshipers packed the Christian Tabernacle. Sitting among the crowd were unfamiliar faces of men who appeared nervous and out of place. That evening, a prayer meeting was held. The night was hot and muggy, but in the distance a summer storm could be heard making its way toward Beijing. The pressures and the heat took their toll on Wang, who drifted off to sleep during the prayer meeting and was only stirred awake at 10:30 in time to close the meeting. After he and Jing-wen had bid the members goodnight, they retired to the parsonage.

In their bedroom, Wang removed his shirt and sat down to read some letters he had recently received. Jingwen thought she heard a noise on the roof, so she went out to investigate. She entered the hall and found herself face to face with a police officer armed with a pistol. He stifled her before she could cry out, sat her down on a chair, and handcuffed her. Meanwhile, Wang continued to read his mail. "Don't move!" he suddenly heard behind him. Wang turned slowly to find two police officers in his room, one with a gun trained on him. Several other policemen quickly entered the room, and an arrest warrant was presented to Wang as the others began to search the room.

By the time Wang was cuffed and led downstairs, Jingwen was nowhere to be seen. The thunderstorm was rolling in swiftly as Wang was led into the courtyard, where some thirty officers milled about. Upset, Wang asked where his wife was. The officers replied that she had been arrested and taken away. Wang began to cry out for help and yelled, "False arrest!" To stifle his cries, the police officers threw a cloak over him, knocking off his glasses in the process. Then they hustled him to an awaiting vehicle and quickly drove off. They removed the cloak in the vehicle, but Wang could hardly see a thing without his glasses. With the rain now pounding hard against the windshield, he lost all orientation as to where he was being taken.

Eventually the vehicle pulled up to a building, and Wang was escorted into the dingy hallway to a cell already filled with men. The prisoners were sleeping on "kongs," cement slabs heated during the winter by coal. Wang noted that there were not enough kongs for the prisoners, so they had to double or triple up, making sleep difficult. Wang, however, had little time to reflect on his situation. Shortly a guard appeared at the cell and escorted him to a room where a senior officer seated behind a desk awaited him.

Angry and upset, Wang immediately demanded to know where they had taken Jingwen and why they, as law-abiding citizens, had been arrested. The officer sternly retorted, "You are no longer a citizen but my prisoner, and you are not free to question me, but you will answer my questions." At that point the officer ordered the guard to return Wang to his cell.

Concern for Jingwen and his church members filled Wang with anxiety. He had reason for concern. Not only had Jingwen been arrested and would remain in jail for over a year, but from Beijing to Guangzhou in southeast China over twenty of Wang's friends and associates had been arrested as part of a larger security sweep to break the back of not only his independent church but also those churches, church leaders, and colleagues who had resisted joining the TSPM.[3]

Unable to sleep in the cramped, hot cell, Wang wrestled with the storm raging within even as his mind raced to plot his next move. What charges could they bring against him? He had not broken any laws, or had he? Certainly opposing the TSPM was not a crime, he reasoned, even if it had put him at odds with the government. The key was to address the government's concern by ending his hostility and active opposition to the TSPM—even if that meant losing his independence. This, he determined, would satisfy the government and end this nightmare as quickly as possible.

The next day the guard escorted him back to the interrogation officer. Before the officer spoke, Wang seized the initiative. "I have opposed the Three-Self Movement," he conceded. "Further, because the government backs the Three-Self, my opposition has offended the Chinese Communist Party."[4] "This was not right," Wang admitted, "because the Three-Self Movement is not unreasonable." Although Wang knew this was a lie, he believed it just enough to spring the trap he had gotten himself into. The interrogator looked at Wang coolly and asked, "Is this all you have to offer?" Baffled, Wang asked, "What do you want me to confess?" Wang's interrogator pressed the issue: "Are you or are you not opposed to the Three-Self Movement?" "I am opposed," Wang replied, "but that is a religious question and not a crime; opposing the Three-Self offends no law of the state." Closing the trap, the interrogator let his next words sink in: "That is where you are wrong; opposing the Three-Self Movement is a crime."

These words paralyzed Wang with fear. His clever scheme had backfired; he had openly confessed to a crime. Worse, the lie had exposed his fear. In the hands of his captors, that fear would be exploited until he eventually cracked. Thus began the slow unraveling of Wang Mingdao. He was returned to his cell to stew in his predicament. Not surprisingly, no peace awaited him there. His cellmates continually harassed him. At night he could not sleep—if anxiety did not keep him awake, the two prisoners who slept on either side of him did. They would bump him or make noise to wake him. Wang complained, but they either ignored him or offered excuses that they were only dreaming or rolling over. During the day, they badgered Wang by discussing his crimes and his likely execution as a counterrevolutionary.

Such talk terrified Wang and only increased his dread and weariness between the daily interrogation sessions. These grew more intense and could last hours. Interrogation typically began with a series of seemingly unrelated and innocuous questions. Though Wang tried to concentrate and be careful, all too often he found that he had incriminated himself before he realized what his examiners were trying to pin on him. On one occasion they asked Wang about a man who had worked at his church. Before the revolution the man had been a provincial secretary of the Kuomintang. Wang admitted that the man had worked at the church but noted that this was only after the man had renounced his previous affiliation. At the time, Wang had been careful to register the man's presence with the Beijing Security Bureau, who had cleared his working with the church. The man moved on but was later arrested and executed as a spy of the Kuomintang. When the interrogators asked if Wang was certain that the man had not spied while working for the church, Wang confessed in exasperation that he had no idea. The interrogator then informed Wang that he had just confessed to a capital offense: aiding and abetting an enemy of the state.

Slowly and meticulously the interrogators broke down Wang physically, psychologically, and spiritually. In the end, by April 1956, he confessed to the following crimes.

1. He had opposed the Three-Self Movement.
2. He refused participation of his church in patriotic campaigns.
3. He had aided and abetted an enemy of the state.
4. He had advocated Christian pacifism.
5. He had encouraged noncooperation with the government.
6. He had disrupted civil harmony between Christians and non-Christians.
7. He had impugned Y. T. Wu, calling him a "false prophet" and an "unbeliever."
8. He had castigated the Three-Self Reform Movement as a "government prop."
9. He had preached against divorce even though it was allowed by law.[5]

With these crimes confessed, the threat of possible execution loomed over Wang even as his cellmates harassed him all the more. Meanwhile, though they had all they needed to hang Wang, his inquisitors turned the screws ever tighter prodding Wang onward to their desired goal. Finally, after nine months of grilling, the interrogators cracked open the door of a possible reprieve. They suggested that if Wang were willing to confess his crimes publicly, the government might be lenient. By this time, Wang was willing to agree to anything to end his torment.

Nonetheless, now began the tedious process of exacting Wang's confession. Given a pen and paper, Wang was instructed to write out a full confession of his crimes. This Wang did, but soon it was handed back as inadequate and told to write it again. When Wang sought guidance as to what was lacking, his interrogators gave hints but no clear direction. Wang rewrote his confession and again it was handed back. His interrogators said it was better, but still needed to be revised. With each draft the government upped the ante: either requiring Wang to confess more or to confess it differently. Wang didn't realize it at the time, but this process was actually part of his reeducation. It was believed that the writing of draft after draft imbedded in prisoners' consciousness the nature of their counterrevolutionary offenses. Over time, this would purge the prisoners' consciousness of errant views, which then could be replaced with a correct understanding according to Party ideology. In this manner criminals politically and spiritually reformed themselves.

After nearly four months, Wang's confession finally passed muster. The next step in his rehabilitation was to confess his crimes publicly; when and where, however, were not specified. Before his public confession, however, Wang was required to record his confession on tape. Later this tape would be played to Wang's friends and former church members so they could hear for themselves Wang confessing his own crimes. Finally, when all was prepared, the examiners informed Wang that his public confession would be before a gathering of TSPM and government leaders. The three-fold purpose of having Wang confess in this forum was explained as follows: (1) to complete the process of Wang's rehabilitation, (2) to discredit any who might retain sympathy for Wang Mingdao, and (3) to provide a forum by which the TSPM could extend a pardon to Wang and welcome him to join the TSPM. To capitulate before his antagonists in the TSPM was a cruel blow and Wang strenuously objected. Nonetheless, his examiners were insistent and Wang was in no condition to resist their demand. Though the prospect nauseated him, Wang knew that there was only one way out of prison: through self-degradation.

The venue for Wang's public confession, the YMCA headquarters in Beijing, was selected for its theological as well as political significance. For decades Wang had opposed the YMCA and its "liberal" leaders, such as Y. T. Wu. To force him to recant at this hall and to beg for mercy from the very leaders he had labeled "false prophets" represented triumph for the TSPM and humiliation for Wang Mingdao.

The confession was scheduled for Sunday September 30, 1956, more than a year since Wang and Jingwen had been imprisoned. Wang entered the hall filled with over one hundred TSPM and government officials. Wang was led to the stage and faced the crowd as the emcee announced, "Wang Mingdao has returned, been reformed and agreed to join the Three-Self Church. Please welcome him."[6] Wang's head remained bowed and his limbs trembled as he read out his confession. Wang was filled with fear, anger, and frustration; truly, this capitulation was the nadir of the nightmare his life had become.[7] When he was finished, Wang sat down while a TSPM official officially received Wang's confession, recognized his transformation, and thanked the government for their patience toward, leniency with, and rehabilitation of Wang Mingdao. Afterward, Wang returned to the jail, but soon after was released, along with Jingwen, to return to the parsonage. Next door the church sat dark and silent, closed and sealed by the Public Security Bureau.[8]

Wang Mingdao's torment, however, continued. Shaken by the confession, Wang hardly spoke. Various visitors and officials visited Wang and Jingwen, urging them to make a clean break with the past and to become active in the TSPM. Wang did not respond. Because Jingwen was physically ill due to the strain of her imprisonment, they attended no church. Haunted by the events of the last year, Wang was thought by some to have suffered a nervous breakdown. He was overheard crying out that he was "Judas" and observed behaving erratically. Jingwen feared that he might take his life, as his father had, should his despair grow too great. She warned those pressuring him to fulfill his vow to join the TSPM that they might push him over the edge. Seeing that his suicide would look bad, they backed off for a time.

Still Wang felt trapped. He knew that if he refused to join a Three-Self church, he would be put back in jail; on the other hand, he could not stomach joining the TSPM. Knowing that the excuse of ill health could not last for long, Wang resolved to visit a Three-Self church, but when Sunday arrived, he simply could not carry through with his plans. Soon the badgering for Wang and Jingwen to join the TSPM resumed and steadily grew more intense. Finally, seven months after their release, Wang and Jingwen were rearrested. Wang was brought before the magistrate who had originally approved his release. Asked why he had failed to join the TSPM, Wang replied, "I have erred greatly. I made a vow to be trustworthy and to be a man of my word, but I failed with my friends and now with the government. . . . To break a vow between friends is one thing, but to break one's vow to the government is a crime."[9] It was obvious that Wang would never join the TSPM, so his crimes were reinstated, and he and Jingwen were sentenced to fifteen years of hard labor.

After Wang Mingdao's second arrest, his friends, confidants, and followers gave up any hope of his eventual return. A few joined the TSPM, but most formed clandestine cells meeting in homes, where they could worship apart from official TSPM churches. These home meetings, or house churches, only represented a small fraction of the Protestants in 1956, but subsequent events transformed these small beginnings into today's enormous house-church movement.

Prior to the arrest of Wang Mingdao, the presence of dissenters had forced the TSPM to pacify as best they could the fears of conservative pastors and leaders. By adopting the Protestant mantra "in essentials unity, in nonessentials diversity" and by changing the name from "Three-Self Reform Movement" to "Three-Self Patriotic Movement," they convinced many that joining the TSPM was a political necessity that would not affect doctrine, liturgy, or polity. However, after Wang Mingdao's arrest and the elimination or dispersal of Protestant dissent, ideology asserted itself once again. By 1958, all doctrine, liturgy, and polity were unified. Churches outside of major urban centers were closed and reduced to a mere handful in the major cities. This was justified at the time as "an expression of Chinese Christians' long cherished hope for unity and a contribution to the nation as represented by the more economical use of resources."[10] This only made sense if "pastors were parasites upon society and that church buildings were public resources going to waste. The inevitable result was the drafting of pastors for labor, and the freeing of as many churches as possible to turn over to the government."[11]

Thus in the two years following Wang's arrest, the official TSPM had become the empty shell just as Wang had predicted in "Truth or

Poison." Only a decade later even the shell was swept away with the Great Cultural Revolution that outlawed all religious observance and eliminated even official religious organizations. Nonetheless, the church survived in dispersed house fellowships just beyond the sight of the wary public security apparatus of the government. Furthermore, they carried with them the memory of the arrest and abuse of Christians such as Wang Mingdao. These memories seared into their consciousness a distrust and enmity towards the TSPM and its leaders that continues down to the present.

The Voice from behind the Curtain: The Government Speaks

Throughout the conflict, the government remained a silent but ever-present force. Content to remain in the shadows, it first used the TSPM to express its will and put pressure on Wang Mingdao to join the fold of the united front through the TSPM. Wang's obstinacy forced the government's hand and so he was arrested. Nonetheless, this tells us little as to why the government felt so threatened by a fifty-six year old pacifist preacher that it not only arrested and imprisoned him but coerced his public contrition before his adversaries. Close reading of Wang's confession provides many answers, for in it one finds not simply acknowledgment of his "crimes" but a calculated recounting of his resistance from the government's perspective. Though Wang Mingdao wrote the words and recited them at his confession, careful examination of his words allows us to glimpse past Wang Mingdao to the motivation and concern of the government that was content to direct this perverse shadow-play from the anonymity of the wings.

Ideological Conversion

"I am a counter-revolutionary," Wang's confession began. In this singular classification the confession captured the essence of Wang's defiance. As a "counter-revolutionary," he had attempted to divide the nation when others sought to unify it. Wang continued:

I cried out that "believers should not be yoked together with unbelievers" and urged believers to separate themselves from unbelievers.
I even preached that Christians are those who break with the crowd;
as a result many believers became peculiar people who could not cooperate with others, and who thus failed to make the proper contribution to our nation and society. Actually believers and unbelievers are
different only in respect to religious faith and should practice mutual
honor. In our opposition to imperialism, in our patriotic activities, in
our building of a socialist society, it is imperative that we unite and
work together.[12]

Whereas, TSPM and Party leaders insisted that identity was
national, political, and ethnic,[13] Wang had insisted that the church
was a "peculiar people" who should be distinct spiritually and institutionally. Thus Wang's confession reestablished the proper order
by ensuring that religious identity be subordinate to "nation and
society."

This led Wang to recognize the danger of his former deviance.
Instead of joining in "opposition to imperialism," Wang's insistence
upon a "peculiar people" had led him to deconstruct the ideology of
the state as anti-Christian and antigospel, putting him and his church
in direct opposition to the plans and purposes of the state to unify
the nation through ideological remolding. Thus Wang confessed:

When the purge of counter-revolutionaries started I should have led
my congregation to support this movement; I should have encouraged
doubtful persons to make a clean breast of their past. Not only did I
fail to do this but I misrepresented the Government by saying it was
using the movement to attack Christians. . . . In all this affair I suspected the Government of attacking religion and persecuting preachers. . . . In all these things I did not stand on the side of the people but
on the side against the people and many Christians because of me took
the same attitude.[14]

After his arrest, imprisonment, and reeducation, Wang's confession
professed that the government did not attack religion or persecute
preachers. Although this doublespeak might at first appear farci-
cal—a brutalized Wang confessing that the state did not persecute

preachers—here Wang's confession carried a blunt message. By forcing Wang to confess what he and even his audience knew was a lie, his confession testified to the power of the government to dominate the words and actions of even one of its most incorrigible dissidents. Vaclav Havel, the dissident Czech playwright who himself was forced to confess counterrevolutionary crimes against his will, explains the power and function of such "mystifications":

> Individuals need not believe all these mystifications, but they must behave as though they did, or they must at least tolerate them in silence, or get along well with those who work with them. For this reason, however, they must *live within a lie*. They need not accept the lie. It is enough for them to have accepted their life with it and in it. For by this very fact, individuals confirm the system, fulfill the system, make the system, *are* the system.[15]

This theater of the absurd where a beaten and broken Wang Mingdao confessed his sins upon his adversary's stage was not a matter of assent but of subjugation; his contrition confirmed the utter futility of resistance. His liberty was assured so long as in word and deed he behaved as if his penance were sincere. Once his actions, however, denied his confession, he was rearrested and imprisoned.

Repentance and the Mercy of the Government

Wang ended his confession with appropriate gratitude to the authorities for patiently bringing him to a true knowledge of himself and for being released into true Christian service.

> I wish to express my genuine thanks to the Government for the teaching . . . they have given me. They have enabled me to see my past errors. Because of the magnanimous treatment which I have received, I am determined to lead Christian believers in obeying the laws, in supporting all Government policies and plans. . . . Although I cannot make up for all previous losses, yet shall I do my best to recover lost ground and to become a truly patriotic and society loving preacher.[16]

This conversion was made possible by the government's saving grace, which was neatly summed up in an editorial attached to the published edition of Wang's confession in *Tian Feng*.

> We denounced the old Wang Mingdao as a counter-revolutionary. We thank the Government for their leniency with him considering his crimes. But if we honestly confess our sins, they will certainly be forgiven (Proverbs 28:13); so we hope all fellow Christians will lovingly help Wang Mingdao to continue his awakening and identify himself more completely with the people. And we hope that Wang Mingdao will make this confession a starting point from which to rid his mind completely of all imperialist poisons and so make up for all past errors. We welcome Wang Mingdao to join us in the Christian patriotic anti-imperialism fellowship and in the zealous reconstruction of the Chinese Church.[17]

The conversion of Wang's "old *anthropos*" flowed from the mercy and grace of "the Government and their leniency" (cf. Rom. 6:6–11). Wang's confession and repentance allowed the government to forgive him and to purify him of all unrighteousness (cf. 1 John 1:9). With conversion came regeneration and a new life as Wang joined the congregation of "the people." Finally, it was the nation that placed before the convert and the purified church their true mission: "the Christian patriotic anti-imperialism fellowship and . . . the zealous reconstruction of the Chinese Church." For Wang Mingdao, following Christ and following the state were now one.

Ties that Bind

At Wang's arrest and confession lie the headwaters where the church of China divides. Further, the church divides according to two very different tales as to the nature of the church. These two tales parallel the tale of Wang's resistance on the one hand and his confession on the other. Although both are tales of one man, they are vastly different. The first is a tale of defiance and suffering whereby the Christian seeks to live in integrity in spite of the powerful political forces arrayed against him. Here the Spirit is recognized in the power to resist and suffer in order that another sovereignty might be revealed apart from the secular order. The other is a tale of subjugation to the tide of historical progress, where in the hurly-burly of life one conforms to the Spirit at work in the progressive ideology of the nation. In this tale, the one who resists the Spirit of progress resists the Spirit of God and, until reformed, suffers the consequence of his own bullheadedness. Just as these two different tales describe the resistance of Wang Mingdao, so they describe the divided church in China to this day.

SIX

Underwriting Persecution

It may not be entirely wrong therefore to interpret the persecution
of Wang as the judgment of history on a theological point of view,
and on a theology that did not allow for the betterment of the society
of man.[1]

Ng Lee-ming

Reports of Wang Mingdao's arrest and imprisonment tore through
an international Christian community still reeling from the
abrupt end of nearly a century and a half of Protestant Missions
and over four centuries of Roman Catholic missions in China. With
serious divisions between Church leaders and ex-missionaries having already surfaced over the conflict between Wang Mingdao and
the TSPM, word of his incarceration added fuel to the controversy.

Evangelical Condemnation

For some, the treatment of Wang Mingdao was a harbinger of the
end of Christianity in China. Despite assurances that the Communists allowed freedom of religion, Wang's arrest and imprisonment was
hard evidence to the contrary. For these critics of Communism, Wang's

treatment revealed the true antipathy of the government toward Christianity and its intent to wipe it from the face of China.

Leslie Lyall, a career missionary with the China Inland Mission and a prolific writer on the church in China, reflected these sentiments. For Lyall, Wang Mingdao and Y. T. Wu were respective champions in a cosmic battle between Christianity and Communism. In Lyall's view:

> Throughout the world today—and nowhere more evident than China—the great red dragon confronts the Church of Christ. The age-long war in the heavenly places is speeding to its climax (v. 7). Satan, the deceiver, confusing men with his specious ideologies and attractive cults, has been cast out into the earth as a defeated foe (vv. 9, 10).[2]

Describing him as "more Communist than Christian," Lyall charged Y. T. Wu with leading this vanguard against the church. Lyall had been suspicious of YMCA leaders such as Wu from the early 1930s. He rightly perceived that the Communists had slowly infiltrated the ranks of the sympathetic leadership of the YMCA and YWCA. Thus, it was no surprise when Y. T. Wu was pegged to lead the Three-Self Movement. In the face of this reality, the idea that the church remained independent and free was ludicrous.[3] As Lyall noted:

> In plain words Mr. Wu states that the Three-self Movement is not now and never has been a free or spontaneous expression of the Church's life. He declares it to be the creation of the Communist Party, to be directed at the highest level by the Communist Party carrying the intentions of the Communist Party.[4]

One man, in Lyall's view, had resisted this subjugation: Wang Mingdao, defender and martyr of the true church in Communist China. Wang's refusal to compromise had pierced Y. T. Wu and the Three-Self Movement's façade of lies and manipulation to expose the true nature of Communism. According to Lyall:

> Wang Mingdao from his biblical standpoint saw very clearly from the beginning the true nature of Communism. He was convinced that compromise was not the way to glorify God nor save the Church.[5]

Accordingly, Wang was arrested because he stood in the way of the Communist Party's efforts to manipulate, corrupt, and eventually destroy Christianity in China. For Lyall, Wang's suffering symbolized courageous resistance to the insidious evil of Communism.

> Wang Mingdao was the chief thorn in the side of the Three-Self Movement because he represented all that they opposed. He, above everyone else, stood in the way of their attaining their goal of a united Church. And very naturally he became the main target of their attacks. If they could break down his resistance, then the back of all resistance in the Chinese Church would be broken. Through Mr. Wang's notable stand, he has become to the world a symbol of courageous resistance to the Communist tyranny and its pathetic puppets.[6]

In spite of these strong statements, this view of Wang Mingdao as staunchly anti-Communist, widely shared by evangelicals with an interest in China, was Lyall's own creation. In reality, Wang was silent on Communism both before and after 1949. Independence from the TSPM had political implications, to be sure, but Wang's ethos was drawn from Scripture and doctrine. His resistance to the TSPM was consistent with his resistance to foreign missionaries, denominations, and the Japanese. For Wang, the church best represented Jesus Christ when it hearkened to sound doctrine and Scripture, but it was led astray by lesser institutional or ideological sirens.

Paradoxically, Lyall's vindication validated the charges of Wang's adversaries, namely, that Wang was a counterrevolutionary at heart. Once Wang's doctrinal concerns are replaced by cold war rhetoric, there can be no room for Christian dissent. This is of critical importance even to this day. Many evangelical supporters of the house churches view the divided nature of Christianity in China according to the axis of socialism versus democracy. This allows no ecclesial or social space in which the house churches might exist within the current political framework even as they retain their ability to govern their own affairs and oversee their mission and message. Unlike many who champion him, Wang had no desire to see the government overthrown, and he would have chastised as idolatry those who see salvation in representative liberal democracy. Wang's concern was to preserve the church that it might retain its doctrinal integrity in a fallen world. He would have refused to submit to the political strait-jacket Lyall provided in cold war ideology.

Liberal Protestants roundly criticized Lyall's stark assessment of the conflict for being too narrow and impractical, given China's social-ist reality. By championing Wang's purported anti-Communism, Lyall needlessly shattered the body of Christ upon the shoals of political ideology. Lyall's "either Christianity or Communism" requirement placed Chinese Christians in the untenable position of deciding between being good Christians or good citizens. Rather than being condemned, the liberals argued that the TSPM should be commended for making the cultural adjustment necessary for Christianity to sur-vive, to be faithful, and to serve the nation.

Over the next three decades, this criticism of the evangelical posi-tion and support for the TSPM would gradually become the position of the mainline Protestant churches. At the same time, Lyall's account of the true significance of Wang Mingdao underwrote evangelical suspicions of Chinese Communism and the TSPM. This divide played itself out in debates extending from church lobbies to the halls of the United States Congress. On the one hand, evangelicals accused liberals of being "soft" on China by defending or ignoring the plight of house Christians in China. On the other hand, liberal Protestants dismissed such claims as overblown, noting that the TSPM offered an alternative for lawful Christian expression in China. Driven by political ideological concerns, however, this debate too often lost sight of the issues that divided the church in the first place. If given a chance, one could offer a different framework, one that might point a way out of the current quagmire.

Protestant Liberalism and the Judgment of God

"A revolution is no dinner party," Mao wrote, and given epochal revolutionary struggle that transformed China, he argued it was not surprising that some suffered so that the masses might prosper. For defenders of the revolution and the TSPM, this perspective explained the arrest and detention of stubborn individuals such as Wang Mingdao. What others viewed as "persecution," they argued, was better understood as the "judgment of God" upon a church that had failed to keep pace with the political movements of the day. For example, David Paton wrote:

> God's judgment today is being executed upon His Church by political movements that are anti-Christian. Of this almost worldwide movement the Communists are the spearhead. . . . It is the Communists of whom the West is scared, and the Communists who appear to be the instruments of the wrath and therefore—since the two can never be finally separated—the mercy of God.[7]

Viewed from this perspective, the Three-Self Church was wise to keep in step with the political movements that were sweeping their land. Unlike many in the West who resisted such progress, they were realizing the great ends of the Social Gospel that liberal Protestant missionaries had sought to bring to China's shores. Rather than condemn the revolution, the Anglican David Paton felt that it was time for Christians hear God's word in the revolution.

> It should not surprise us to find that God is addressing us in the political and social revolutions at its heart, which so disturb the life of the Church. One of our main themes indeed is that the ending of the missionary era in China by Communist *force majeure* is to be understood as the execution of the will of God, albeit through those who not only do not recognize Him but deny His existence.[8]

It is against this backdrop that liberal Protestantism understood the events unfolding in China, including Wang Mingdao's arrest and imprisonment. Given the inexorable tide of social and political progress in revolutionary China, they argued that it was not surprising Wang's irrelevant message and recalcitrant stand should be swept aside before the tide of history. By needlessly dividing Christians when unity was required to address the deep social ills, Wang was hindering progress. As Lam Wing-hung argued, this was not merely a political problem but a theological problem inherent in Wang Mingdao's message that rested upon an impractical "cultural dualism." Thus, according to Lam:

> In Wang's theology we see the constant dichotomy between faith and reason, the Church and the world, sons of God and enemies of God, individual gospel and social gospel. This cultural dualism has naturally led to a form of monastic retreat from the world in turmoil and . . . self-righteousness in social relationships.[9]

Wang's insistence upon distinguishing the church from fallen society represented a flight from reality and thus an irrelevant and otherworldly gospel of little value. In Lam's judgment, "Christianity as Wang understood it would at best be tolerated and ignored by the powers that be, and at worst be persecuted."[10] Blind to the larger arena of God's social redemption, Wang had become an obstruction and a reactionary force to the political liberation movements of his day.

The root of his shortsightedness was his overemphasis on salvation at the expense of a more comprehensive doctrine of creation. Thus Lam argued:

> The shortcoming of his position is that Wang has an incomplete theology of culture and was still living in the mentality of the nineteenth century missionary. Although Wang may be strong in his doctrine of salvation, he has largely neglected the doctrine of creation which precedes the redemptive schedule of God.[11]

According to Lam, Wang's failure lay in his failure to have adequate theology of creation and culture. The assumption being that since national and cultural identity precede salvation, emphasis and distinction based on redemption should be secondary to questions of social progress, and national reconstruction. This neglect of the doctrine of creation resulted in Wang's emphasis on the church as the locus of God's salvific activity and led him to obstruct the political movements of the day. Thus, according to Ng Lee-Ming, Wang Mingdao's persecution was no accident but rather judgment upon a truncated gospel not attuned to the "Creator of nature and Governor of history as well as to the Spirit immanent in creation and in the Christian community."[12] Or, as Ng Lee-ming concluded:

> It may not be entirely wrong to interpret the persecution of Wang *as the judgment of history* on a theological point of view, and on a theology that did not allow for the betterment of society and of man.[13]

According to this view, Wang Mingdao is not God's martyr, the defender of the church, or even an anti-Communist crusader, but rather as one found guilty before the bar of divine justice. The common thread in these latter assessments was the doctrine of creation fused with progressive political movement. Accordingly, the punishment of recalcitrant evangelicals who obstructed political liberation became understandable. This perspective thus underwrote the persecution of individuals such as Wang Mingdao as divine judgment.

Seeking a Balance

Between the evangelical and liberal wings of Protestantism, Francis P. Jones, a Methodist who worked in China from 1915–1951, sought a middle way between the contending wings of Western Christendom. Jones wished neither to justify the imprisonment of Wang Mingdao nor to condemn the TSPM outright. Rather, Jones argued that the conflict between Wang Mingdao and the leadership of the TSPM exemplified the age-old conflict in Christendom between the official state churches and the pious sects. For Jones, Wang Mingdao was "another George Fox, battling for freedom of conscience in the face of totalitarian demands of the state Church," while Y. T. Wu was an "Oliver Cromwell . . . who looks upon the imprisonment of such an individualist as a pious act."[14]

Jones criticized both wings of Protestantism for questioning the faith of either Y. T. Wu or Wang Mingdao. According to Jones, each man represented hard choices that Christians have faced throughout history, each with its corresponding virtues and vices. On the one hand, Wang's sectarian position maintained the purity of the church at the cost of "espousing . . . ideals that have no chance of acceptance by the body politic." On the other hand, engaged and realistic, Y. T. Wu's embrace of socialism came only at the dilution of his Christian ideals.

Jones held these two adversarial and irreconcilable positions in tension within the larger framework of the church. By separating the validity of Y. T. Wu's and Wang Mingdao's faith from their actions, Jones believed that the true character of their faith was revealed in their Christian sincerity. Thus, Jones at one moment described the denunciation, arrest, and imprisonment of Wang Mingdao as "one of the most clear-cut cases of religious persecution that has come out of China," then a few pages later offered this on Y. T. Wu:

> Wu preached a sermon in Peking in the summer of 1952, a sermon that closed with these words, "Fundamental religion is this—to stand like children before the infinite majesty of God, to adore, depend, and obey." That is a language that speaks to my heart, and I recognize in the speaker a fellow-heir to the promises of Christ.[15]

Jones's apparent equivocation might seem puzzling, unless one recognizes the factors that led him to seek this middle way. During this debate, Lyall, Paton, and Jones were all Protestants who to some degree viewed themselves within the larger tent of the World Council of Churches. However, squabbles over Communism threatened to break asunder hard-fought ecumenical unity. By cutting a middle path between the pre-positional political views of Leslie Lyall and David Paton, Jones believed he had discovered a third way above the prepositional politics dividing ecumenical Protestantism.

Paradoxically, however, Jones's third way made political alignment definitive for the church. In Jones's view, neither state church nor sect were biblically or doctrinally derived, but determined solely in their relationship to the nation. Thus, "sect" was not defined in reference to a larger ecclesial body, nor did "state church" refer to Christendom in any way. Rather, these terms were solely defined according to modern political alignments. As such, the institution and function of the church became arbitrary and inconsequential to faith. Instead, like a chameleon endlessly changing hue to avoid predators, the task of the church was simply to survive in whatever institutional framework suited it at the time.[16]

Wang Mingdao's Imprisonment—and Release

Ironically, although Wang Mingdao's imprisonment was at the center of these debates, he knew nothing of them. He and Jingwen were separated and imprisoned in Beijing. Wang was granted permission to write Jingwen, but her warden refused her permission to read his correspondence. This was never conveyed to Wang, who continued to write even though he received no reply.

Jingwen, however, caught glimpses of Wang on several occasions, since their prisons were located next to each other. In the prison yard one day, Jingwen noticed a group of male prisoners being led outside and recognized Wang. Fearful he would be punished, she stifled an impulse to yell out. The same scenario played itself out several times during the months of their imprisonment. Jingwen noted that Wang had become frail and ill and feared for his health. Wang, however, never saw Jingwen; his eyesight was too poor to see that great a distance.

Over the next six years Wang's health deteriorated. Malnourished and depressed, he also struggled with failing eyesight and diminished hearing. In 1963 he grew very weak and began to vomit blood. He was placed in the prison infirmary and nearly died. His condition stabilized after a period of rest, but this did not necessarily please him. Sick and depressed, Wang wished to die. His ministry was finished. He was a convicted criminal. Worst of all, the humiliation of his confession haunted him. Weak, emaciated, and depressed, he received at the infirmary the government's coup de grace: a government notification that upon review his sentence had been extended to life imprisonment.

What use was there to go on living, he asked? It would be better just to die and be over with it. Then, in the midst of his despair, a passage of Scripture that had struck him as a young man came to mind:

> But as for me, I will look to the LORD,
> I will wait for the God of my salvation;
> my God will hear me.

Do not rejoice over me, O my enemy;
when I fall, I shall rise;
when I sit in darkness,
the LORD will be a light to me.

I must bear the indignation of the LORD,
because I have sinned against him (Mic. 7:7–9a).

For the first time in six years, Wang felt a surge of hope—but even more than hope. Through this passage Wang came to grips with all that had transpired since the night of his arrest. Trapped in the unrelenting vice of fear, his spirit had withered. It was fear that had given birth to the lie that had ensnared him the night of his arrest. Fear had let interrogators manipulate his words so as to fashion a gibbet of his own making. Fear had placed him upon the stage of his humiliation and allowed those who had destroyed his life and ministry to gloat over his demise. Now, with a life sentence before him and his health nearly gone, the shackles of fear fell off and a surge of courage renewed him. Flooded with a peace that overwhelmed his dark night of incarceration, he felt released to live out a radical liberation.

Wang's health improved and, though sixty-three years old, his feistiness soon returned. He took pen and paper and began to write page after page about his arrest and imprisonment. In these prison papers, he retracted his previous confession, pronounced his imprisonment unlawful and unjust, and presented his current detention in light of the saints who had been imprisoned, not for criminal acts, but for openly preaching the gospel.

Wang's revived spirit would soon be tested. As soon as he was released from the infirmary, he was put back on a work crew. However, because he did not regard himself as a criminal, he refused to do prison labor. As punishment, Wang was placed in a narrow confinement cell just large enough to allow him to sit. After four months of solitary confinement, he was transferred to Datong Prison in Shanxi province, a hard-labor penitentiary where he would spend the next five years in prison.

Deep in the belly of China's labor camps was perhaps the safest place for Wang. Outside, China was in turmoil as the nation suffered through wave after wave of political campaigns. In the Anti-Rightist Campaign of the late 1950s, intellectuals who only a year earlier had been encouraged to offer criticism were now brutalized and punished severely. The Great Leap Forward followed. Mao challenged the nation to catch up with the West industrially through mass mobilization. Peasants left their fields and produced tons of worthless iron. Millions would die in the ensuing famine. Mao's rivals in the Communist Party used the debacle of the Great Leap Forward to clip his wings, reducing his role to ceremonial functions. Mao bided his time but rode back to power on the wave of young people who flooded Tiananmen Square in 1967, sparking the debacle of the Great Cultural Revolution. Mao elevated his wife Jiang Qing to the heights of power and punished his political rivals.

Meanwhile, the nation descended into massive social and cultural anarchy. Universities were shut down. All religion and religious practices were banned, and religious books burned. TSPM leaders were arrested or sent to the countryside to learn from the laboring peasants. Temples, churches, and mosques were turned into factories, and an incalculable measure of China's historical legacy and treasures were destroyed as elements of the "Four Olds" (old ideology, old thought, old habits, old customs) that needed to be eliminated. Eleven million "red guards" fanned out across the nation handing out summary justice. Finally, Mao, having sufficiently "revolutionized" the nation, called in the army to restore order.

For Wang, the Cultural Revolution meant increased denunciation sessions in which incorrigible elements were to be reformed. Wang's inquisitors were known among the prisoners as the "gang of nine." They submitted prisoners to endless interrogation sessions and tortured them if their answers were not what the interrogators desired. In one session, Wang was asked to comment on Jiang Qing, Mao's wife. Wang chided Jiang Qing's acid tongue for having labeled the former President Liu Shao Chi's wife a prostitute. Wang's flippant answer drew handcuffs that were not removed for months. During the ensuing interrogation sessions Wang would be dragged from the room by his cuffs and forced to bend over in the painful "jet" position. At other times, he was made to run in circles with his hands shackled until he fell—sometimes against the walls. Bruised and bloody, Wang would be wrenched to his feet by his hair. Wang's cuffs were not removed for five months, but he refused to yield. He insisted he was not a criminal but was suffering for his faith. Finally, his interrogators admitted that he was too old and too stubborn to be reformed. Wang affirmed this, and his cuffs were removed.

In 1968 Wang Mingdao was transferred to Yingying Prison in Shanxi province. By the early 1970s, the conditions for Wang and the other prisoners improved, and they were even allowed more freedom. Wang was granted permission to correspond with Jingwen, who had been released from prison in 1970. She had moved to Shanghai to live with their son Tianduo and his wife. The improvement of conditions paralleled the thaw in tensions between China and the Western nations after Richard Nixon's visit to China in 1972. Mao's death in 1976 only accelerated the pace of change. When Hua Guofang, Mao's successor, came to power, he released many of the former leaders imprisoned during the Cultural Revolution and arrested Jiang Qing and her associates. One of those released was Deng Xiaoping. Deng quickly rose to power and immediately instituted massive reforms. Colleges and universities were reopened, agricultural communes were broken up, and industry was given top priority to help China rebuild out of the rubble of the Cultural Revolution. To rally people to his cause, Deng allowed more freedom of speech, even allowing for a time a "Democracy Wall" in Beijing where dissent could be presented. In addition, political prisoners and prisoners of conscience were released, some of them having been imprisoned since the 1950s.

In January 1979, Wang Mingdao's son Tianduo received a telegram to come fetch his father, now seventy-nine, who was to be released from Yingying Prison. Tianduo traveled six days by train to Yingying and, upon meeting the warden, went with him to Wang's cell. Wang recognized his son but had no idea why he was there. When Tianduo gave him the news, Wang responded, "I am not leaving. You go tell Ma that I am fine and that I am staying right here." The official was shocked and interjected, "Your son has come all the way from Shanghai to take you back to Shanghai. You must go with him." Wang remained adamant: "I cannot leave here until my affairs have been properly settled. I am not a criminal and have been held for over twenty years for what are not crimes but solely because of my faith."[17] The perplexed official tried to cajole Wang: "Why pursue this matter? Prison is an awful place for an old man like you." Wang retorted, "Having rotted here for twenty years, don't you think I know how awful this place is? But I'm used to it, and I'm staying." "Then I command you to leave!" ordered the Warden." "If you wish me to leave," Wang replied, "I require three things of the government: first, an admission that my arrest was in error; second, that my sentencing was unjustified; and third, an apology for twenty years of wrongful imprisonment—then I will leave."

That evening Tianduo returned to Wang's cell. Realizing that Tianduo could not return to Shanghai dutifully without him, Wang reluctantly agreed to leave. The next day Wang was summoned to the warden's office to sign the necessary papers for release. The papers read, "prisoner Wang Mingdao having received a life sentence for counterrevolutionary crimes, that sentence is now commuted to time served and is hereby released." Wang refused to sign anything that described him as a criminal. Wang informed his son that there was nothing to be done but for him to return to Shanghai and for Wang to return to his cell. Tianduo took the next train back to Shanghai.

Given Wang's intransigence, the warden took a different tack. In consideration of Wang's age and frailty, he had Wang moved to a facility outside the prison. Here prisoners were allowed to come and go freely. What Wang did not know was that this was a temporary facility soon to be shut down. It was only when other prisoners informed him of this that he discovered he had been tricked. He could hardly demand entry back into prison, and an eighty-year-old man would never survive alone in Shanxi, so Wang sent a telegram to Tianduo informing him to come for him. Unable to come, Tianduo sent an old friend of Wang's from Beijing to meet Wang and to accompany him to Shanghai. In this way Wang was released without an apology.

News of Wang's release spread quickly both in and out of China. Soon a steady stream of visitors began to appear at Wang's small apartment. First to visit were Chinese Christians who came to honor Wang Mingdao. Later, foreign visitors and dignitaries arrived, many from Taiwan and Hong Kong, where his books continued to be published and widely read by Chinese Christians outside Mainland China. Western

Christians also came, including Billy Graham, who stated that he came to China for two purposes: to visit the birthplace of his wife and to visit Wang Mingdao.

Wang did not mince words with those who visited. He spoke of his false arrest and of being imprisoned for twenty years simply because of his faith in God and his refusal to join the TSPM. He remained adamantly opposed to the Three-Self Church and refused to speak or have any dealings with any of its representatives.

At a time when China was attempting to portray its best face to the world, the steady stream of foreign visitors to Wang's apartment was a bit of an embarrassment. Thus, in 1985 the Public Security Bureau paid Wang a visit. They asked for a list of his visitors' names and details of their conversations. Wang refused. They warned him that such defiance was unwise for a convicted counterrevolutionary. Wang informed them that he was not a criminal and that he had been imprisoned on false charges. If they wished to arrest and imprison him, he could not stop them, but they would still get no information from him. Getting nowhere, they gave up and left him alone.

Renewal and Division

After Wang's return, he found himself once again at odds with his old rivals over a church divided. The government knew that Christianity was spreading. The few churches they had allowed to open had lines of people waiting outside to get in every Sunday, but even this represented only the tip of the iceberg. The United Front Work Department institutions, established in the 1950s for oversight and control, had all been cleared away during the Cultural Revolution. To address this vacuum and in order to rally support for its economic and political reforms, the government recalled former TSPM leaders and pastors to reestablish the TSPM. Their job was to reopen churches, to reestablish and communicate the nation's religious policy, and, naturally, to oversee and control the burgeoning Christian renewal in China.

The situation, however, had changed remarkably in twenty years. During the 1950s the TSPM had driven all its rivals from the field either by co-opting them into the TSPM or by leaving it to the government to remove them. As we have noted, however, leftist pressure that eliminated all vestiges of Christianity actually served to create an unseen rival: the house fellowships. The government had banned such gatherings, but the size and flexibility of these groups made them difficult to discover and root out.

With the end of the Cultural Revolution, these house fellowships were uniquely situated to expand during the gradual relaxation of state pressure during early 1970s. For individuals trying to piece together their broken lives out of the abyss of China's "Dark Decade," these fellowships helped heal the scars and address the anger, cynicism, and despair that ran deep through the nation. Their numbers swelled as Christians grew bolder and shared their faith with others. Even the national newspapers noted with alarm the spread of "Christianity fever" both in the cities and in the countryside. Areas once labeled "religion-free" only a decade before now boasted tens of thousands confessing to be Christians. It was reported that even some Communist Party officials had secretly converted.

Such growth startled the government, so it handed the TSPM the difficult task of wooing these independent fellowships back into the fold. This task was complicated, however, due to the legacy of the 1950s. Moreover, the specter of Wang Mingdao now holding court in Shanghai haunted their efforts. To help deflect criticism, a parallel China Christian Council was established, not merely to serve as a political bridge to the government, but primarily to address the needs of the churches. Further, under the guise of criticizing the excesses of the Cultural Revolution, admissions to mistakes were recognized and attempts were made to distance the TSPM from the arrest and imprisonment of figures such as Wang Mingdao.

Such moves convinced many to rejoin the TSPM and to register their house fellowships. This not only granted official legitimacy but also helped many to recover church buildings and confiscated land. However, others who wished to join were unable to do so because provincial and local officials were often uninformed of changes in religious policy. These officials would stymie or even close down what they regarded as illegal religious activity. Other officials refused to allow groups to register, fearing that too many churches and Christians in their district might reflect badly on their leadership.

Still, despite these governmental moves to calm Christian fears, millions of Christians refused to have anything to do with the TSPM. Its leaders were the very men and women who had led the reeducation campaigns, closed the churches, denounced independent leaders, and acclaimed the arrest and imprisonment of faithful Christians. Those who refused union saw the TSPM as little more than an organization to control, manipulate, and stifle the Christian renewal sweeping China. They took special note of rules forbidding evangelism and healing services, two elements central to the spread of Christianity.

Thus the animosity and cynicism that Wang Mingdao had felt toward the TSPM was reflected in the divided church of China. In 1989, the TSPM appealed for Wang Mingdao to bury the hatchet and to join the TSPM. Given Wang's sentiments, the appeal published in a TSPM journal article would appear to have been directed, not to Wang Mingdao, but to the wider church that remained wary of the TSPM. The article distanced the TSPM and its leadership from Wang's arrest and imprisonment as well as other abuses of the 1950s.

The article paralleled other moves by the TSPM leadership to be more outspoken on behalf of the rights of Christians. TSPM leaders were more vocal in their defense of the rights of Christians and critical of the government when these were abused. When the government began to pressure home fellowships to register with the government, K. H. Ting criticized these actions. He argued that, given the climate of distrust that already existed, such moves only alienated groups already suspicious of government interference. In the end, however, Christianity remained deeply divided in China through the mid-1980s.

Rekindling an Old Controversy

Into this divide Christians from the West entered. The exponential growth of the Chinese church was deemed miraculous given the church's suppression during the Cultural Revolution. There was a hunger within Western Christians to discover the secret to the Chinese church's survival and growth. As might be expected, evangelicals established ties with independent house-church leaders. For example, evangelicals helped meet the severe need for Bibles and Christian education materials that the unprecedented growth of the Chinese church had created. Although some printing was going on in Nanjing, this slow trickle could not touch the need for Bibles in China. Further, collecting Bibles required official registration, something that many house churches would not risk. Thus, evangelical groups began to smuggle Bibles and Christian education materials into China.[18]

Reports of foreigners smuggling Bibles into China greatly disturbed the TSPM leaders. Foreign meddling, especially in matters of religion, was (and is) still a sensitive matter. As a response, the TSPM worked with its friends in mainline Protestant denominations in the West to denounce such activity and to help China set up modern printing presses to meet the Christian population's need for Bibles and to develop Christian education materials written and printed in China.

Books and articles soon appeared either championing the cause of the underground house churches or the TSPM churches. Those sympathetic to the house churches wrote of continued persecution and the insidious presence of political ideology remaining in the TSPM churches. Those supporting the TSPM wrote of its accomplishments and championed its practical theology, which had been effective in preserving Christianity through forty difficult years even as they condemned efforts by conservative evangelicals that undermined the policies of the government and the TSPM.

The most notable of these latter works is Philip Wickeri's *Seeking the Common Ground: Protestant Christianity, the Three-Self Movement and China's United Front*. Wickeri's expansive account of the Chinese church from "liberation" to the present details and defends the TSPM's endeavor to establish a niche for Christianity within an avowedly Marxist society and an officially atheist country. Naturally, such an account had to address the legacy of the 1950s, when the movement was born and the controversial denunciations, arrests, and imprisonment of dissenters took place. If the formation of the TSPM was simply a matter of removing Western influence and of establishing a truly independent and Chinese church, why were leaders of independent indigenous churches such as Wang Mingdao harassed, arrested, and imprisoned?

In an interesting twist, considering Wickeri's defense of the TSPM is ostensibly theological,[19] Wickeri turns to Mao's "theory of contradictions" to justify and explain the TSPM's rhetoric and actions towards those outside its ranks. As will be recalled, Mao's "theory of contradictions" held there were two types of reaction to the CCP's united front. On the right were counterrevolutionaries and reactionaries who were antagonistic to the revolution. On the left were doctrinaire Marxists who rejected the gradualism of the united-front in favor of a more radical imposition of orthodox Marxism. Equilibrium could only be gained through "struggle" against these two reactions that threatened the unity and stability of the nation. In the same manner, Wickeri in his chapter "Rejection and Renewal" views independent sects and evangelicals doctrinally opposed to the TSPM under the title "Rejection from the Right."[20] Those with "ultra-leftist tendencies" that radicalized the TSPM in the late 1950s Wickeri places under the title "Rejection from the Left."[21] In the center stands the TSPM, a sort of Christian united-front, represented by the current and former leadership of the TSPM who overcame the right and left contradictions in order to establish the TSPM that remains in place to this day.[22]

After dismissing radical sects on the "right" that were too theologically unorthodox, divisive, and otherworldly to be acceptable either too the new regime or the vast majority of Christians, Wickeri turns to the more troubling figure of Wang Mingdao. Though "belligerently fundamentalist and militantly independent"[23] Wickeri concedes that Wang's faith was basically orthodox and that the criminal case against him was flimsy, revealing the "inadequacy of legal safeguards for Chinese citizens in the early years of the People's Republic."[24] That said, Wickeri notes that the theological case against Wang had to do with his uncompromising refusal to join the TSPM and his narrow intolerance that were neither theologically nor pragmatically justified in a society where the "fundamentals of faith did not set the terms for human existence."[25]

Beneath the harsh rhetoric that characterized the conflict between the TSPM and Wang Mingdao, Wickeri discerns three valid criticisms of Wang Mingdao.[26] First, Wang's contention based on 2 Corinthians 6:14–18, that Christians should not be "yoked" with "unbelievers," confused benign institutional union with the biblical command that believers should not be joined in "sinful behavior" or join in worship with other religions.

Closely related to this was the TSPM's second criticism that because it was clear that union with the TSPM was patriotic and not doctrinal, Wang's refusal put him not only at odds with the TSPM but with the government. Bringing these two criticisms together, Wickeri upholds the view of the TSPM that Christians burying doctrinal axes to serve the noble cause of social progress was hardly immoral but to be commended. On the other hand, Wickeri argues that Wang's rejection of patriotic union in the TSPM was neither biblically nor pragmatically merited in a society desperate for unity and harmony. More ominously, because union with the TSPM was politically enjoined, this made Wang's dissent subject to the laws of the state. According to Wickeri:

> Wang was asking that he and his following be ignored, but this in itself involves a social and political understanding which was neither mandated by the Bible nor acceptable in a socialist context. In urging his followers to separate themselves from the world, Wang Mingdao seemed to be ignoring that it was a world in which they had to go on living and working.[27]

In the final valid criticism of Wang Mingdao, Wickeri argues that Wang's intolerance flowed from his "extremely narrow interpretation of the gospel." This led to Wang's failure to extend "mutual respect" to the leaders of the TSPM and his venomous labeling of TSPM leaders as "false prophets," "non-Christians," and "Disciples of Judas."[28] Wickeri contrasts this to the "theological comprehensiveness" of the leaders of the TSPM who argued that Christian love required tolerance and "mutual respect" with regard to differences of opinion about Scripture and doctrine. This "theological comprehensiveness" allowed for the union of evangelicals and modernists in the common ground of national patriotism that Wickeri commends as the great accomplishment of the TSPM.

Given Wickeri's argument above, it is not surprising he remains silent on the doctrinal issues Wang raised in "We Because of Faith." According to Wickeri, questioning the faith of those who deny the divinity of Christ is not only narrow, if pressed too far, it was political and thus a criminal offense in the world where Christians "lived and worked." Nonetheless, Wickeri's wooden categorizations of Wang Mingdao as narrow and fundamentalist and the TSPM leadership as tolerant and theologically comprehensive aside, were we to press Wang's doctrinal concerns upon Wickeri himself it would reveal the shakiness of Wickeri's own theological foundation. Wickeri does not address the issues Wang raised because if he did he would be forced to admit that the leaders he defends had serious doubts as to the divinity of Christ, the inspiration and authority of Scripture, the objective character of the atonement, etc. As Wang noted, his detractors did not respond because they did not believe. They didn't dare openly declare their unbelief for fear it would shatter the fragile alliance of modernists and evangelicals in the TSPM. For Wang, however, it wasn't narrow, intolerant, or disrespectful to declare someone who didn't believe in the basic doctrines of Christianity an unbeliever. It was simply a true or false statement that stood on its own merit. Thus, for Wang, faith in Christ was a matter of belief, not national patriotism, and to suggest otherwise was ludicrous. Wang argued this way because he believed that Scripture and doctrine addressed matters of truth and thus could not be treated simply as doctrinal preference on which Christians were free to disagree.

In the end, the TSPM no less than Wang Mingdao upheld the narrowness of truth. They simply differed over the nature of that truth and their willingness or unwillingness to endorse coercion to establish it. As a pacifist, Wang rejected coercion. This is in stark contrast to Wickeri. While Wickeri's "theological comprehensiveness" extends as far as doctrinal difference, just beneath its velvet glove lies the iron truth of secular ideology. Hard, narrow, and intolerant, the truth of united-front ideology allowed no dissent. In upholding this truth, Wickeri can at once denigrate Wang's belligerent insistence on faith in Jesus Christ's resurrection even as he explains away a life sentence of hard labor for an old man who had committed no crime. This is because Wickeri's vaunted tolerance only applies to theology and doctrine. When it comes to challenging political ideology, arrest and imprisonment are understandable.

Indeed, the more one examines Wickeri's critique of Wang Mingdao, the more Wickeri's unstable secular theological foundations are forced to the surface. Wickeri's methodological reliance upon Mao's "theory of contradictions" doesn't bear the weight of careful scrutiny. Wickeri views both conservative evangelicals on the "right" who resisted incorporation into the TSPM as well as radicals on the "left" who sought to eliminate the TSPM as "sectarian," not in terms of a greater theological concord, but solely in terms of the "common ground" of the united front. Accordingly, Wickeri can at one moment recognize the relative orthodoxy of Wang's theology yet at the same time dismiss Wang's stand as sectarian, theologically naïve, and unjustified. The great accomplishment of the TSPM, according to Wickeri, was the discovery of the church's true identity within the common ground of patriotism revealed in the embrace of political ideology. But, we must ask, at what cost?

The serpentine course of the People's Republic of China under the leadership of the Communist Party from 1949 onward, dutifully lauded at each turn by the TSPM, hardly affirms the wisdom that the church should establish its "common ground" in the political ideology of the state. What Wickeri views as errors on the left were not viewed as errors at the time but rather the true course of the revolution. Attacks on intellectuals and "progressive" Christian leaders during the Anti-Rightist Movement were extolled by the TSPM leadership as the true path of "liberation." Wickeri champions the status quo of the TSPM reestablished under Deng Xiaoping's reforms that brought to an end the folly of the Great Cultural Revolution. Nonetheless, only a year after Wickeri's book was published, thousands flooded Tiananmen Square from across the nation to express their frustration with the leadership of the Communist Party. They, in turn, were crushed by military intervention that shocked not only the world but the Chinese people themselves, who have tasted bitterness more than most over the last forty years.

I retell the painful history of China since 1949 not to compound the frustrations of the Chinese people, nor to critique the Chinese Communist Party, which, despite setbacks, has done much to improve life in China. Rather, going back over this sordid period only underscores what Wang Mingdao clearly saw. That once the foundation of the church is established on the common ground of patriotism and political ideology as opposed to Scripture and sound doctrine, the church is constrained to praise the actions of those in power as righteousness itself. Only by a narrative held apart from the self-justifying rhetoric of political ideology can the church gain the high . moral, spiritual, and intellectual ground necessary to offer society prophetic insight and guidance.

 SEVEN

Christian Suffering

For what more glorious or more felicitous could happen to any man
from the divine condescension than, undaunted before the very exe-
cutioners, to confess the Lord God; than to confess Christ, the Son of
God, among the various refined tortures of the cruel secular power.

letter of the presbyters Moses, Maximus, and their companions, in
Cyprian, *Letters*, 31, nos. 3, 6[1]

The contentious and tangled history of the church in China during the last fifty years continues to provoke argument and provide fodder for the political and ecclesiastical battles joined from
church halls up to the bastions of state power.[2] What is often not
noted, however, is how the subtext of modern nationalism has shaped
these debates and the historical and theological assessments that have
flowed from them. Because national identity is so inextricably intertwined in modern existence, all too often its hidden assumptions and
theological reflexes go unnoticed. As we have seen, however, the
resistance, conflict, arrest, and confession of Wang Mingdao forced
those assumptions and reflexes to the surface and in so doing revealed
the fissure between nationalism and religious faith in China that has
continued down to the present.

Unlike Europe, where modern nationalism evolved over several centuries, the notion of China as a unified national community is a creation of the twentieth century. As Benedict Anderson has suggested, for most of the non-Western world the concept of "nation" is largely an "imagined community," imposed rather than evolved.[3] Nonetheless, rather than diminishing the pull and power of modern nationalism over countries like China, it has intensified it. As Arif Dirlik has pointed out:

> Imagined the national community may be . . . but it may be all the more revolutionary for being imaginary, for nationalist political ideology since its origins in Europe in the sixteenth and seventeenth centuries has called forth the reorganization of societies globally into nations. This in turn has provoked a revolutionary reconceptualization of political legitimacy and a reconstitution of political space internally to create nations. We need only to remember that over the last two centuries, even the most despotic states have excused their despotism by recourse to national interest, which those who have struggled against despotism have countered by asserting their rights as citizens—and alternative conceptions of national interest.[4]

In large measure, the desire for a "revolutionary reconceptualization of political legitimacy and a reconstitution of political space" gave rise to the May Fourth Movement in China as well as the Kuomintang (Nationalist) and Communist parties of China. Nonetheless, those who pursued modern nationalism soon found themselves in conflict with nationalism's chief rival: the religious consciousness of the Chinese people. This led to the subsequent Anti-Christian Movement, the campaigns against Popular Religion waged by Nationalists in the late 1920s, the elimination of religious dissent in the 1950s, and finally the banning of all religion during the Cultural Revolution.

The cause of this rivalry lies in the tension that religious consciousness has posed to the imposition of nationalism in China. For millennia in China, clan, land, and ancestral filial piety grounded communal and individual identity. For nationalists, both Kuomintang and Communist, these arcane ancestral ties were the source of China's endemic weakness: a cultural legacy inhibiting the urgent task of developing a national consciousness. They believed only a forceful disenchanting of the Chinese people of their superstitions through imposition of a secular national identity could secure the vigor and progress of the nation. The problem was how to overcome the resistance of "the people" themselves, who felt no need to be remade in the image of the nation. As Prasenjit Duara has noted:

> The campaigns which sought to destroy popular religion did not merely seek to secure a representation of the people, but tried to remake real people so they could conform to the representation. It was a forced, violent remaking, the implications of which extended beyond religion.[5]

Here lies the political root of Wang Mingdao's forced confession. As Wang himself confessed, he was a counterrevolutionary due to his complete lack of "national and racial consciousness."[6] His reliance upon Scripture and doctrine tore at the inner coherence and legitimacy of national consciousness. In the end this defiance led him to reject the indoctrination of his church frustrating the desire of the TSPM and the government for all Christians to find their common ground and identity in the nation.

Although the above provides the secular political reasoning behind Wang Mingdao's censure, arrest and imprisonment, it does not explain the theological judgments leveled against him. As we have shown, these judgments have also been caught up in the maelstrom of national consciousness and political ideology. What sets these judgments apart from their secular counterparts is their appeal to "the judgment of history." Accordingly, for Y. T. Wu, David Paton, and Ng Lee-Ming, the justification of the establishment of the TSPM, the indoctrination movement, and the imprisonment of Wang Mingdao derive from a theological perspective that views social and political progress as the vanguard of God's Spirit. The upshot of this assumption has been the dismissal of Wang's doctrinal and biblical concerns as at best irrelevant and at worst directly at odds with Spirit of God at work in the progress of the nation.

On closer examination, the difference between the theological judgment of Wang Mingdao and his theological critics is one of interpretation. For Wang Mingdao, Scripture and doctrine formed the critical lens by which the church should construe modern existence and gain its distinctive insight by which to engage secular society through the Word of God. In contrast, secular reason, culture, conscience, and national progress form the critical lens of Wang's critics. Accordingly, secular society presents an identity for and an authority to the church. Wang's failure to defer to that authority led to "the judgment of history on a theological point of view, and on a theology that did not allow for the betterment of the society of man."[7]

It is at this point that the conflict between Wang Mingdao and the TSPM leaves its parochial setting and enters the wider theological conflict over biblical inspiration and authority that has been waged over much of the last century between modernists and evangelicals. Indeed, it is precisely here that Wang's stand provides crucial insight. While the battle over the Bible between modernists and fundamentalists has largely centered on the nature of Scripture and revelation, Wang Mingdao's stand brings to the fore the relationship between biblical authority and the church in the modern age.

Modernism, Liberalism, and Political Theology

The twentieth-century evangelical movement did not arise so much as a response to errant interpretations of Scripture or mistaken doctrine but as a reaction to what many Christians regarded as a dangerous shift away from the primacy of Scripture toward other avenues of revelation and truth. For example, the appeals of modernists such as Shailer Matthews to the authority of "scientific, historical and social method in [the] understanding and applying of evangelical Christianity" did not strike evangelicals as modern thought supplementing the gospel but the subordination of the gospel to authorities other than Scripture.[8] Indeed, as J. I. Packer has noted, evangelicals have distinguished themselves from modernists in their insistence that the Bible should have "complete and final authority over the Church as a self-contained, self-interpreting revelation from God. But this is what Evangelicals are concerned above all to maintain.

What Scripture says, God says; and what God says in Scripture is to be the rule of faith and life in His Church."⁹

Accordingly, the battle between modernists and evangelicals has not been merely a war of words and doctrine but rather a profound battle over the church and its relationship to the surrounding milieu in the modern age. Modernists believed that dogmatic insistence on Scripture and doctrine left Christianity in the shackles of obscurantism. To suitably address critical issues facing humankind in an enlightened, scientific and technological age, modernists sought to mitigate what they regarded as the *irrational* dogmatic authority of Scripture, tradition, and doctrine by *rational* appeals to national and cultural progress based on the authority of science, reason, and conscience. As George Marsden has noted:

> "Modernism" in fact, meant first of all the adaptation of religious ideas to modern culture. So when the modernists affirmed the immanence of God, they characteristically meant that God is revealed in cultural development. The corollary was that human society is moving toward realization of the kingdom of God. These principles and especially this last, represented new versions of postmillennialism; the spiritual progress of the kingdom could be seen in the progress of culture, especially democratic cultures in Europe and America.¹⁰

As we have seen, this understanding led to the theological judgment of Y. T. Wu as well as David Paton that it was the duty of the church both theologically and practically to keep up with the Spirit of God being revealed in the progress of secular society. To keep pace required a "non-dogmatic, non-ecclesiastical, non-sacramental, and non-legalistic"¹¹ understanding of faith wherein the truth of God could be discovered through science, social theory, and human progress. Modernists argued only such a fresh understanding of gospel would allow the church to come to grips for with the calamities facing modern society. This was poignantly put by Paul Althaus:

> To every age the one eternal gospel must be proclaimed. But to every age it has to be proclaimed differently, as an answer to the specific questions of that age. . . . At the time of the Reformation the question of

salvation was the question of deliverance from guilt, of peace with God. . . . Today we are an utterly political species and our quest for "salvation" comes alive in the political dimension. People of our day are not concerned about peace with God, but with overcoming political calamity in the broadest sense—the mortal distress of a people, the destruction of the national community, the freedom of the *Volk* for its own life, the fulfillment of its particular mission. If that is the key question for our age, the gospel must be preached to it in terms of its "political" concept: the kingdom of God, the Lordship of God.[12]

Althaus's concern resonates deeply with that of Y. T. Wu and Philip Wickeri. All three agree that, if Christianity is to find its home and to be relevant in the modern age, it should take its cues from the social, political, and ideological structures and forces bringing about progressive change.

The political theology Althaus championed found fertile ground in the academic religious establishment of 1920s and 1930s Germany. For those who embraced political theology, it represented the next evolutionary stage in theology for it extended Protestant liberalism's concern for conscience and science to the progressive movements of liberation and social reconstruction. As such, its defenders viewed it as a necessary correction to archaic and inept evangelical piety that had little to offer the German people in a time of crisis. Thus, Emanuel Hirsch would chide Karl Barth that the job of the theologian was to "read God's real intention for creation out of the formative and creative forces of history . . . There is no other way to inscribe sacrifice for state and nation on the hearts of our *Volk* than by awakening faith in the Lord of history, who testifies in conscience that he is alive."[13]

Hirsch viewed Barth's contention, that "we must keep to God's revelation in Jesus Christ, as He is witnessed to us in Holy Scripture,"[14] as hopelessly biblicist. Hirsch retorted:

Christ and God are not to be found in the Bible alone. . . . Faith in Christ must become concrete in the acceptance and refashioning of the definite historical situation. Therefore the "German Christians" ask for a new concreteness in the Christian direction of life in the present situation and task of the German people.[15]

Here Hirsch captured the critical distinction. Rather than Scripture shaping life, faith must be fashioned according to the "definite historical situation." The key to relevancy in the modern age was to understand and fashion faith according to the progressive political movements of the day. Thus, in a passage reminiscent of the Christian Manifesto,[16] Hirsch wrote of the Nationalist Socialist Movement in Germany:

> Now the change has come without the help of the Church. It has come with the primitiveness and impetuosity with which the will to self-preservation is accustomed to break through in a people threatened at its roots. The Church must now have open eyes for that which in this new turning is in accord with the will of God. She must help the government in its difficult work, must stimulate reverence and faithfulness in regard to blood, and must encourage the will to have children in all classes of our people and especially among the educated, where one finds the least inclination thereto.[17]

In short, political theology looked at the progressive political movements of the day and saw therein the Spirit of God. The duty of the church was to find its identity therein for only in this manner could it participate positively to the unfolding of God's kingdom on earth. Evangelical insistence upon Scripture and doctrine only frustrated this endeavor by questioning the fusion of Christian and nationalist identity. Further, evangelical emphasis on separation of church and society or believer and unbeliever impeded social and political progress as the church became a reactionary force opposed to the progressive revolutions sweeping the twentieth century. In the view of modernists, evangelical rejection of political theology consigned Christianity to reactionary irrelevancy at odds with the tide of history and subject to its ultimate judgment.

Confusing God and Nation

Karl Barth, who contended with Althaus and Hirsch's "political theology," wrote of the danger that the establishment of an "*ordo* of the nation" based on a preceding order of creation posed to the church:

> there is then erected an *ordo* of nation and nationality which is supposed to be immanent in human nature and therefore to be originally and finally determinative and binding. . . . This twofold discovery shows itself to be illegitimate and in the most concrete sense of the term heretical. . . . it inevitably introduces a foreign deity, a national god from whom this specific command proceeds and who has created man in accordance with it.[18]

Barth's concerns reflect what we noted in Wang's confession where nation and nationality, as the essence of human nature, was seen as "determinative and binding" as the essence of created human nature.

Barth recognized that this, the creative act of the nation, was heretical, for it required that the believer view nation and nationality as having precedence over God and identity in Christ through faith. It logically follows that Barth's concern for Christian identity would challenge Lam Wing-hung's criticism of Wang Mingdao. Lam argued that Wang's distinction between believers and unbelievers failed to recognize that the "doctrine of creation . . . precedes the redemptive schedule of God."[19] The gist of Lam's criticism is that the citizen's national identity precedes and thus trumps the later redemptive distinction between believer and unbeliever. In the view of Barth and Wang Mingdao, this presumption of national identity in fact belies a "foreign deity, a national god . . . who has created man in accordance with it." In response to this modern heresy, Barth reiterated the distinction between an evangelical understanding of God and the national god of political theology in order to reestablish the true "proclamation of the Christian Church":

> The Father of Jesus Christ, who as such is the Creator, cannot be recognized as this national god. It is not He who gives this command or has created man in accordance with it. This national god is thus a strange god, his service a sacrificing on alien altars and therefore this doctrine is a false doctrine which can only disturb and disrupt the proclamation of the Christian Church, and therefore spell ruin rather

than salvation for the world. It is for this reason that we must avoid maintaining and teaching it.[20]

Wang Mingdao's rejection of the TSPM arose out of the same concern. The church was not to submit to any organizing principle outside of that sanctioned by Scripture and doctrine. Accordingly, only by understanding church and society according to the redemptive order of God that distinguishes between faith and unbelief can the true nature of the created order and the consequences of the fall be properly understood. This is why both Wang and Barth rejected the notion that the various configurations of fallen human governance were revelatory of God. As the flawed creations of flawed human beings, they were unworthy of the honor and worship reserved for God alone.

The Church and Society

Wang's distinction between believers and unbelievers and his commitment to the primacy of Scripture and doctrine, critics claimed, blinded him to the possibility of social improvement through progressive secular political movements. In this view, unless one interprets Scripture according to a secular narrative, one grows hopelessly out of touch with the real issues individuals, societies, and nations face. Wang, however, exposed the fallacy of this criticism. In "Truth or Poison?" he showed that by subordinating God's will, Christian identity, and institutional authority to social or political progress, the church was gutted of its presence, power, and authority. In its place was established a formal, ceremonial institution whose only purpose was to sanction, or secure submission to, the political and social power brokers of society. The church of political theology was a church in name only, at odds with a community formed in accord with its faithful reading and interpretation of Scripture.

Wang's insistence that the fundamentals of faith establish the norm of human existence allowed him the critical distance necessary to hold both the church and society accountable. Supplied by faith in the dogmatic authority of Scripture and the prophetic nature of the church, this stance gave real presence and power to God's church. The penetrating simplicity of Wang's arguments, which cut through the subterfuge and indirection of his opponents, remain the source of their continued validity when they are compared to the political theology of his antagonists. Because political theology rides on the prevailing winds of political fortune, the arguments raised against Wang fifty years ago now drip with the hackneyed and irrelevant prose of Marxist dogma. Thus it is not surprising that the positions of his adversaries championed in the late 1940s and early 1950s were swallowed long ago in the leviathan of the revolution. The opposite is true of the works of Wang Mingdao. Although Wang was chastised at the time as irrelevant and escapist, his works remain in publication and the issues Wang Mingdao raised fifty years ago continue to be relevant in the church in China today.

Human Identity and Christian Faith

The primacy and integrity of Christian identity lay at the heart of Wang's dissent. For Christian modernists and the Chinese government, this obstructed the path of progress founded in national identity. To combat Wang's stance, his opponents reduced his Christian identity to the status of a mere "cloak" even as they fixed his true essence in terms of political ideology. Wang's failure to concede his Christian identity lay at the root not only of his arrest and imprisonment but also at the theological salvos that have been directed at him ever since. Thus Wickeri writes:

> Anyone who is familiar with the situation will admit that Wang Mingdao was opposed to the principles and policies of the People's Government, and this is the most likely reason for the action taken against him. Yet the theological issue was that of the Christian's relationship to a world in which the fundamentals of faith did not set the terms of human existence.[21]

Wickeri is correct that the theological issue at stake *was* Wang's insistence that the fundamentals of faith do set the terms of human existence particularly for the church. Nonetheless, if the fundamentals of faith are not to set the terms of Christian existence in the world, what should? Wickeri concludes that the social and political milieu ought to set the terms of human existence for Christians as well as non-Christians. Nonetheless, Wickeri's criticism of Wang would just as well apply to Karl Barth and Dietrich Bonhoeffer before the *Wehrmacht*. Wang Mingdao's reasons for refusing to join the TSPM correspond to those stated in the Barmen Declaration, which opposed the "political" union sought by the Nazis and the leadership of the German Evangelical Church:

> In opposition to attempts to establish the unity of the German Evangelical Church by means of false doctrine, by the use of force and insincere practices, the Confessional Synod insists that the unity of the Evangelical churches in Germany can come only from the Word of God in faith through the Holy Spirit. Thus alone is the Church renewed. . . . We reject the false doctrine, as though there were areas of our life in which we would not belong to Jesus Christ, but to other lords—areas in which we would not need justification and sanctification through him.[22]

Wang, like the writers of the Barmen Declaration, questioned the theological legitimacy of "other lords" or "areas [of life] in which we would not need justification and sanctification through him" (Jesus Christ). As the writers of the Barmen Declaration declare, the great sin being foisted upon the church was the state's imposition of the terms of human existence: "We reject the false doctrine, as though the State . . . should and could become the single and totalitarian order of human life, thus fulfilling the Church's vocation as well."[23] The clear assumption of the Barmen Declaration and Wang's defiance of the TSPM was the same, namely, that it was the church's vocation, and not that of the nation-state, to order the life of the church and the believer according to the Word of God. This differs sharply with Wickeri's position, which regards the imposition of a single totalitarian order over an entire nation as simply the given of modern China and resistance to that order as culturally naïve and theologically inadequate.

Moreover, even the latitude of the church recognized in the Barmen Declaration to order the life and worship of believers is constrained by what Scripture actually teaches regarding the divine. As Barth explained in 1935: "We are not free to call anything 'God' which we think divine, but we must keep to God's revelation in Jesus Christ, as He is witnessed to us in Holy Scripture."[24] This view challenges the view of the Christian Manifesto and the writing of David Paton that it was in the progressive political movements of the day wherein the church should seek the divine. Here again, Barth and Wang agree that the divine is to be discerned in and through the church's faithful reading and interpretation of Bible.

Wang argued that, unless the church defines existence according to Scripture and doctrine derived therefrom, the church becomes exactly what the Barmen Declaration also affirmed: an ornamental church that serves to support the ideological myth of "freedom of religion" even as it denies the essence of that freedom. On the other hand, by emphasizing the continuing validity of Scripture to authorize the church, Wang established a real community whose existence, shaped in accordance with the Word, provided an alternative to the narrow imaginings of modern nationalist identity.

Tragically, Western evangelicals, as we noted in Lyall's ideological vindication of Wang Mingdao, have at times shared the modern presumption that political ideology determines true Christian essence. This has led many so-called evangelicals to confuse party affiliation and Christian identity. This was true in Germany at the time of the Barmen Declaration where the great majority of those who considered themselves evangelicals sided with the Nazis in their takeover of the German Protestant churches. This fact, however, does not deny the legitimacy of Barth or Wang's criticism of political theology nor cut its tie from Protestant liberalism and modernism. Rather, it merely reveals the insidious and powerful draw of political ideology and political theology in the modern age.

Gnostic Liberalism and Fundamentalist Relevance

The arrest and imprisonment of Wang Mingdao is strong evidence against the view that the gospel he preached was a type of modern

Gnosticism that attempted to ignore or escape social and political reality. As we have seen, the term *Gnosticism* better describes the faith of "socially relevant" liberals such as Y. T. Wu after 1949. Recasting Christian identity according to political ideology, Wu consigned Christianity to "spiritual needs" and "eternal yearnings," what William James referred to as the "experiences of individual men in their solitude."[25] As Wang pointed out, such a religion offends no one: "Those opposed to God do not hate this kind of Church and they wish to convert the Church to this form, which though it has its worship hall and ceremony, in fact represents the destruction of the Church."[26]

What Wang condemned, the government understood as religion discovering its true features:

> Speaking with Christian leaders in May 1950, Zhou Enlai made this significant statement: "Let religion restore its true features." . . . Socialist countries practiced a policy of religious freedom, gradually restoring religion to its original status as a personal matter while making it part of the ideological beliefs of a portion of the masses. . . . Struggles between the two ideologies are inevitable, but most of them do not slacken their efforts to bring about the good life before their eyes because of their religious faith. They have made an accommodation holding that the pursuit of happiness on "this shore" can be integrated with anticipation of happiness on "the other shore. . . ." In their eyes religion is truth and socialism is truth as well; the two can coexist. In their words, "Love for one's country is identical to love for one's religion."[27]

Once love for one's country becomes identical to love for one's religion, the contradiction between believers and the state vanishes. Wang, however, refused to give such loyalty to the state. Wang rejected the pretension that such loyalty represents. Like the authors of Barmen, he insisted that the church could only be faithful as a prophetic and at times resistant institution within secular society.

The Tide of History and the Suffering of the Church

The demand that the church live under the lordship of Christ and resist all who would attempt to usurp his place as head of the church has, at times, put Christians at odds with those who rule. Although labeled as "escapist" from Barmen to Wang Mingdao, this insistence has been profoundly creative, practical, and relevant. Although Wang Mingdao and other Chinese independent Christian leaders have been criticized for being hopelessly biblicist and belligerently dogmatic, in the end they were the few who challenged the banal conformity embraced by more "enlightened" modernists and liberals when they were all faced with the totalitarian impulses of the nation-state.

What is often missed by modernists who glory in an unabashed relativism is how quickly they conform to whichever way the milieu turns. They have no anchor by which to question the tide of history, trapped as they are to "make its rhythms (their) own, to move within its currents in search of reality, of beauty, of freedom, of justice, that its fervid and perilous flow allows."[28] Instead of discovering a true autonomy free from all the constrictions of authoritative dogma, such individuals find it difficult if not impossible to resist the strong unilinear currents of modern nationalist identity. Thus, it is not surprising that some of the most brilliant twentieth-century theologians have ended up providing the theological justification for some of the most brutal and repressive political regimes in history, as witnessed in the work of Paul Althaus and Emanuel Hirsch.

All too often those with a modernist bent have viewed the persecution and suffering of uncooperative Christians in China as the just penalty for impeding the progress of society. As Y. T. Wu argued:

> The times demand a move forward; if our religion is superstitious, backward, and opposed to the interests of the people, then all that we stand for will be swept away *under the ruthless judgment of history*. It will indeed be tragic if at that time we still think we are being persecuted for righteousness' sake and are bearing the cross of Jesus.[29]

Viewed from this perspective, Wang's imprisonment was not suffering for "righteousness sake" but the "ruthless judgment of history." This parallels recent criticism of Wang Mingdao by Bob Whyte. In a chapter appropriately entitled "The Tide of History," Whyte describes Wang's suffering as "the price paid by a Christianity that had never attempted to take seriously the context in which it was set."[30]

It is doubtful that Whyte would praise Christians in prewar Germany who argued that, if God had given them Hitler, then Hitler they must have. Nonetheless, when it comes to Christians in China he argues that passive acceptance of coercion and manipulation was not only practical but also justified. According to Whyte's logic, Barth and Bonhoeffer should not be lionized for their resistance to the Nazis but rather should be chastised for defending a Christianity that failed "to take seriously the context in which it was set." The total failure of Whyte and Wang's other critics to discuss the relevance of Barmen to theological and political issues in China is telling. Were they to bring up the parallels, they would either have to deny the reasoning behind Barmen, that Christ and not the state is the head of the church, or simply accept the theological inconsistency of their own arguments.

The imposition of political ideology upon Chinese Protestantism was not passive, nor were Wang's arrest, confession, and eventual imprisonment the result of Whyte's inexorable "Tide of History." Rather, they were the government's brutal imposition of political ideology by indoctrination, manipulation, and coercion even as it refused openly to declare or take responsibility for its acts. The most cynical of these acts was the forced confession of Wang Mingdao. This strange parody in which a bullied and broken Wang Mingdao parroted the party line did not happen of itself, but was the deliberative action of those with political and religious authority. In his willingness to suffer, Wang revealed those actions for what they were: not the inexorable tide of history, but the willful and illegitimate persecution of Christian dissent.

Whyte's claims aside, there is nothing to suggest that Wang did not take his context seriously. Wang's resistance was not a failure to grasp his situation but rather a testimony that individuals, communities, and even nations insubordinate to the rule of Christ can move "the tide of history" in evil directions. Indeed, because Wang took his context as seriously as he did, he resisted to the point of suffering twenty years of harsh imprisonment to defy the collective evil being foisted upon the church and the people of China. This is why Wang suffered.

Neither futile nor meaningless, Wang's suffering bore witness to the judgment, and ultimate victory that has echoed down through

Christian history. In early Christianity a *martyr* was one who "witnessed" to the truth through suffering. Christians believed they shared in and thus bore *witness* to Christ's suffering through their own affliction. As such, suffering came to embody the ongoing *martyria* ("witness") of the church. Moreover, just as Christ had been vindicated in the resurrection, so the early church came to understand their own suffering in light of the vindication and the judgment of God. Thus, in the book of Revelation, it is those who "by the blood of the Lamb and by the word of their testimony [*martyrias*] . . . did not cling to life even in the face of death" (12:11) who sit in judgment over those who worshipped idols.[31]

Just as suffering was intricately bound up in what it meant to bear public witness to the lordship of Christ in a hostile world, nearly two millennia later this understanding of Christian witness remains relevant particularly in the case of Wang Mingdao.[32] While others negotiated away their Christian identity before the pressure of the government, Wang's suffering bore testimony to the public character of the church. By refusing to yield to what he regarded as laws against truth, he witnessed to the rule of God on earth. According to this logic, the church suffers when it resists the pretense of the secular powers to place themselves upon their own altars and forget that their authority is only temporal. Suffering is all the more unavoidable when as Christ's representative, the church rejects the use of violence to establish Christ's lawful authority. Instead, as the body of Christ, it is exposed to the violence of dominions and powers that do not recognize the church's authority and proscribe her public presence and mission.

In spite of such brutal treatment, it is in suffering that the public and the eschatological dimensions of the church are most profoundly revealed. Wang suffered because he was unwilling to consign faith to the realm of irrelevance and escape, insisting that right doctrine had public ramifications that could not be avoided. In so doing he incurred the wrath of the government and suffered two decades of harsh imprisonment. Those who would justify the excesses of revolutionary governments as nothing less than the hand of God dismiss Wang's suffering. When compared with more ancient appraisals, however, such modernist assessments only reveal their intellectual and spiritual deformity, for it is neither in the state nor in its brutal treatment of Christians where God is revealed, but in the freedom, judgment, and ultimate victory revealed in those who suffer for Christ.

Such suffering is absurd when the "common ground" of the church is not Christ but the nation. On the other hand, when Christians are willing to suffer rather than subject the church to the *ordo* of the nation, then the cruciform nature of the church is most profoundly revealed. Here lies the significance of the persecution and suffering of Wang Mingdao at the hands of the state and its ongoing relevance to the church of China today. In bearing witness to Christ through twenty years of imprisonment, Wang Mingdao submitted himself to judgment—not to a "judgment of history" rendered by court historians or political theologians but to a judgment rendered by one well acquainted with sorrow and suffering.

Defying Heaven's Mandate

Wang Mingdao and the Divided Church of China

For three millennia China's emperors ruled by *Tianming*, the Heavenly Mandate. This divine fiat sanctioned the emperor to monitor, circumscribe, and, if necessary, eliminate any religious activity that might represent a threat to the imperial throne.[1] Challenging the Heavenly Mandate, whether by active subversion or doctrinal transgression, was tantamount to sedition and ruthlessly put down.[2] Only religious orders willing to bow low before the imperial throne were allowed to exist and flourish.

With the collapse of the Qing Dynasty, the Heavenly Mandate may have passed from view as official state doctrine, but as the arrest and imprisonment of Wang Mingdao revealed, its influence did not.[3] That the rulers of China continue to keep the Mandate's talons firmly affixed upon religious expression in China was revealed in the government's recent demolition of the Falungong cult as thousands were arrested, interrogated, and its leaders imprisoned.

147

Nonetheless, ten years after the death of Wang Mingdao and nearly half a century after his refusal to join the TSPM, millions of Christians worship and fellowship outside of government sanctioned TSPM churches. Thus, though the influence of the Heavenly Mandate remains, by any measure the policies that reflect its concerns have failed. That failure is rooted in the issues Wang raised nearly half a century ago, and until those issues are resolved, Wang Mingdao's legacy will continue to haunt those charged with enforcing Heaven's Mandate.

The Legacy of Wang Mingdao

Up to 1989, two years before Wang's death, pressure upon independent house churches gradually eased. Even TSPM leaders called for official tolerance of Christians meeting outside of registered churches. However, this relative calm soon gave way to the political storm that swept the nation in the spring of 1989 as thousands of students and workers converged upon Beijing. They gathered in Tiananmen Square before the portrait of Mao to protest Communist Party corruption and to demand sweeping political reform. These political tremors exposed deep fissures in the Communist Party, as Zhao Zhiyang, Deng Xiaoping's hand-picked successor, called for Deng and his "old guard" to relinquish power in order that true reform might proceed. Deng countered by arresting Zhao and ordering the army to crush the rebellion. Deng's triumph, however, cost him dearly. To survive, Deng was forced not only to decimate the reformist cadre of leaders he had carefully nurtured to succeed him but also to embrace elders within the Party who despised his reforms and demanded they be shelved indefinitely until the tarnished image of the Party was restored.

Restoring that image in an age of rapid change has not been easy. Justification of the Communist Party's monopoly of political power rests on Marxist-Leninist ideology and the thought of Mao Zedong. At the same time, the embrace of modern economic theory and the drive of top officials to modernize China by riding market capitalism has continued to eviscerate the ranks of true believers in Marxism and Maoist thought within the Party hierarchy. This has created a crisis of legitimacy, as the ideological vacuum has combined with public frustration over widespread official corruption of leading Party members. Even by the Party's own analysis, its perception by the public is at an all-time low. A report issued in early 2001 by a senior adviser to President Jiang Zemin warned of "mounting public anger over inequality, corruption and official aloofness."[4] The report painted a gloomy picture of social unrest manifested in a "growing pattern of large protests, sometimes involving tens of thousands of people."[5]

The decline of ideological purity and the rise of Christianity have galled Party elders, who expected the influence of religion to wither as liberation took hold. With millions of Christians and their numbers growing daily, that is hardly likely. Leaders have also noted with dismay the role that religious dissent played in the dismantling of the Soviet Bloc. Their worst fears were confirmed in an internal document circulated among senior leaders in late 1989. It detailed the erosion of Party support in the countryside due to the spread of "Christianity fever." As Party influence flagged, the churches grew. In some locations, Party prestige had sunk so low that Party cadres paid villagers to join the Party and to attend meetings. In one village, official announcements had to be made from the church pulpit to ensure they reached villagers. For China's old guard, this document bode ill tidings for the Party, which once boasted that it would last ten thousand years. This is why, according to a recent U.S. State Department report, "Communist Party officials . . . perceive unregulated religious gatherings as a potential challenge to their authority, a threat to public order and an alternative to Socialist thought."[6]

In response, the government has turned up the heat on independent house churches, banning all religious meetings outside designated locations. In addition, recently erected independent churches, formerly ignored, have now been razed. Independent pastors, elders, and evangelists are subject to harassment, arrest, or imprisonment. During the year 2001, this policy took a deadly turn, as independent-church members died under interrogation as police sought evidence against their pastor. Moreover, several house-church leaders were sentenced to death as late as January 2002.[7]

In spite of this crackdown, attempts to rein in Christianity have not only failed but also have proven counterproductive. Increased persecution has only forced independent religious groups to become more secretive and thus harder to monitor, even as their suspicion and animosity toward the Communist Party has deepened. This has provided fertile soil for the growth of cults, whose teaching is not subject to the internal controls of doctrinal criticism where faith is practiced openly. Meanwhile, the government's brutal campaign against house churches has drawn the ire of Western leaders and provided fodder for the foreign press and human-rights organizations eager to expose China's shoddy human-rights record.

China's leaders are averse to Western prodding on human-rights issues. Nonetheless, given China's recent entry into the World Trade Organization and China's selection as the site of the 2006 Olympics, there is strong impetus to clean up the nation's image. Thus, in a three-day meeting in Beijing, the seven ruling members of the Politburo Standing Committee discussed easing restrictions on independent religious groups. President Jiang Zemin argued that the "broad masses of believing people" are no longer to be regarded as a threat but contributors to the social fabric of the nation.[8] What effect these pronouncements will actually have is a matter of some debate. Some now expect the government to allow house churches to register as churches separate from the TSPM. Others, however, view Jiang's words as a mere publicity ploy to ease criticism of China at a time they wish to present their best face to the world. Meanwhile, house-church leaders and members remain wary of this apparent olive branch. Burned before, they note that the government has not backed away from death sentences recently handed down.[9]

The Divided Church As Legitimate Concern of the Communist Party

If nothing else, the Communist Party's contradictory messages and actions reveal that the divided church in China is a real concern, but one must ask if that concern is legitimate. The desire to end official corruption by establishing a kingdom of righteousness reverberates down through Chinese history. In this regard, religion has never been a benign force in China. The fecund wombs of religious sects have born many a rebellion with imperial designs. For example, China's most recent rebellious sect drew from Christian roots. As Jesus' "little brother" and the "Son of Heaven in the Period of Great Peace," Hong Xiuquan led a rebellion from 1837–1854 that conquered southern China. The force it took to crush the Taiping Rebellion so exhausted Qing imperial forces that it precipitated their own demise only forty years later. The Taiping misadventure only reinforced what had been the policy of China's dynasts for centuries. To keep religious rivals at bay one should destroy temples, defrock thousands of monks and turn them out of monasteries, and exterminate dangerous sects if one wished to keep a firm grip upon China's imperial Dragon Throne.

Moreover, rebellion festers in China, as in most places, when official corruption is rife. This fact has not been lost on China's current leaders, who have been battling endemic corruption for the last two decades. Several high-ranking Party officials have been publicly exposed for embezzling millions of Yuan; some have even been executed for their crimes. If the cancer of corruption was reserved to the upper echelons of the Communist Party, high profile cases and harsh penalties might surgically remove it. The problem for the Communist Party is that corruption has spread across society. Indeed, the flowering of Christianity in China is in large measure a reaction to the vice that pervades society. Thus, as corruption eats away at the Party, the attraction of Christianity grows.

This has led some in the Party to fear the spread of Christianity. However, those who fear another Christian Hong Xiuquan arising should recognize that his brand of Christianity was ill-informed and heretical. No Christian institutions were available to correct his errant views until it was too late. Such a cult could arise from the underground Christian sects, but if it did it would result from their secretive nature and thus their lack of exposure and correction. Consequently, the current policy actually exacerbates the threat of dangerous cults forming. The solution to this would be for house churches to operate in the open and to allow the government to monitor their beliefs. For this to happen, however, the Chinese government must revisit the issues and policies that led to its conflict with Wang Mingdao, which originally divided the church in China. Until these issues are resolved, the government will find no path out of its current quandary.

Establishing a True Three-Self Policy

Self-Governance

At the heart of Wang Mingdao's dissent from the government-approved TSPM was resistance to government meddling in the affairs of the church. His church had been self-governing, self-supporting, and self-propagating twenty years before the revolution, and Wang simply wanted it to remain so.

Thus, if the government truly seeks out of its current dilemma, it must begin by ending its intrusive meddling into church governance. Churches should be allowed to establish their own government and standards of faith and doctrine. This would entail freedom to establish religious schools that would teach and train their leaders accordingly. Certainly, given the government's concern that churches not advocate the overthrow of the government, this self-governance would have political parameters. However, those parameters should be broad enough to allow self-governance that does not impede house-church Christians from sharing their faith with others. Workable models that exemplify such a policy already exist in other parts of Asia. For example, Taiwan and Singapore require churches to register and monitor what churches believe and teach. Nevertheless, they allow the churches to manage their own affairs with a minimum of interference as long as the churches do not attempt to subvert the government or stir up interreligious antagonism.

Self-Support

Wang Mingdao's pursuit of a church independent of foreign control or meddling paralleled Party concerns to wean China of foreign domination. Ending China's servile status was viewed as necessary for the Chinese people to develop their own institutions and expertise that would ensure stability and growth over the long period. Over the past fifty years, both the nation and the churches have stood up. China is a powerful nation, and the churches are independent, indigenous, and self-supporting.

Ending state oversight of Christianity would merely establish as official policy what is already practiced in the house churches. They do not seek government patronage. Like their Christian forbears in ages past, they recognize that "with the Queen's shilling comes the Queen's command." Moreover, making self-support official policy would actually serve the government. No longer would they need to prop up designated leaders of the churches or direct the business of the churches. This would free the government's hand to attend to more pressing business. Monitoring churches is far less troublesome than running them, and if the house churches were free to surface and worship openly, the task of monitoring would be greatly eased.

Concerns that foreigners and foreign mission bodies would return to dominate the Chinese churches are misplaced. No longer do Christians in Asia or the developing world blindly follow the lead of Western churches. Indeed, lately Asian and African churches have flexed their spiritual and institutional muscles, dictating the direction of international denominational bodies, at times over the objections of their Western counterparts. This was witnessed at the recent Lambeth Conference of Anglican Bishops, where bishops from Asia and Africa overruled their liberal-leaning American and British peers to set the agenda for the worldwide Anglican Church for the next decade.

Given the growth and vigor of Christianity in Asia, and particularly China, that influence will only expand. Reopening the Chinese churches to foreign mission workers and support at this point would only strengthen development and independence. The promise and problems of massive growth will require input and support in theological education and church development. Foreign expertise would help stabilize the Chinese church. Further, open contacts and interaction would serve to influence and to contribute to the growth and depth of Christianity worldwide.

As it stands, the TSPM has largely limited its contact and interaction with the more liberal mainline denominational churches and mission bodies in the West. In many ways this has been a tactical error. Not only has this policy kept the TSPM from influencing the great majority of Protestants in America, it also has cut off the resources Western evangelicals could offer TSPM congregations that are for the most part evangelical in faith and practice.

Self-Propagation

Finally, Wang Mingdao rejected government pressure to interfere with the teaching and practice of sound doctrine. Moves to challenge his distinction between believer and unbeliever represented unacceptable interference into the preserve of the church. This continues to be the major sticking point between the independent house churches and the government. Noninterference in the message and mission of the church, especially in its freedom to share what it regards as the truth of Jesus Christ to non-Christians, is a hallmark of the independent churches. They refuse to join TSPM churches, whose doctrines are reasonably evangelical and orthodox, because the latter are forbidden openly to evangelize. Thus, they view TSPM churches as caged songbirds who only can sing where their master permits. In contrast, China's house churches are resolutely evangelistic. They feel compelled to spread the gospel even if they are hounded for doing so.

Self-propagation will also have positive social and ethical ramifications. Concern for the moral fiber and ethical character of the Chinese people motivates the preaching of the house churches and swells their ranks. For house churches, the gospel is good medicine that combats the contagion of decadent materialism and corruption even as it strengthens virtue and character. As with Wang Mingdao, a strong commitment to ethical behavior and discipline has defined Christianity in the house churches. Therefore, given China's ethical problems, the government ought to embrace this influence, not fear it.

The Benefits of a Truly Three-Self Policy

The brutal treatment of Christians in China puts pressure on Western governmental officials to respond. China, in turn, bristles at foreign interference and reflexively defends its dignity. Allowing independent churches to govern, support, and propagate their faith without undue government interference would remove this irritating thorn from important bilateral relations.

Allowing relative autonomy and responsibility in the churches would also provide a needed forum in China for its people to exercise freedom responsibly. Moving church governance from the government-controlled TSPM to independent church organizations would provide a place where Christians could develop the experience needed to govern and oversee institutions and organizations. Spreading the burdens and privileges of governance would stabilize society by providing outlets of expression in a venue that is not directly political in nature.

As it now stands, the government must spend time and energy locating, infiltrating, and then breaking up house-church groups. Not only is this time-consuming and expensive, but by any measure it has failed miserably. In contrast, should the government allow true open self-governance of the churches, it would enable the state to monitor the activity, doctrine, and faith of the churches far more easily and openly. Rather than hiding from the authorities, house churches could operate openly, thus exposing their teaching and activity to public scrutiny. It would also reduce the threat of dangerous cult activity, as the churches develop their own internal controls of education and training to identify, isolate, and address errant teaching.

For the churches, self-government would mean the long nightmare of the last fifty years would finally have ended. The contentious issues that led Wang Mingdao to resist the government would essentially be removed. This would allow the churches to spend their energy on the difficult problems that exponential growth represents. Instead of looking over their shoulders, they could focus on establishing institutions to train qualified clergy and lay leaders. Cults, heresy, ignorance, and dangerous practices are as much a problem for the churches as they are for the government. Allowing Christians to mind their own back-yards would relieve the government of some of their own work.

Finally, designating millions of otherwise good resourceful citizens as "enemies of the state" is not wise policy but rather a failed relic of another era that should be jettisoned for the benefit of all. Jiang Zemin's call to recognize nonregistered Christians would appear to acknowledge that fact. Nonetheless, those sentiments will not result in effective policy until the government is ready to recognize in private, if not in public, its errors in the handling of Wang Mingdao's resistance.

What Role for the Three-Self Church?

The end of the TSPM's officially sanctioned monopoly on Protestant affairs would be good news not only for the house churches but also for the union of churches found within the TSPM. Granted, there would be some initial difficulties. Independent churches would use the TSPM's legacy, ongoing resentment toward the TSPM, and latent frustration to woo Christians away from TSPM churches. It is further likely that factions within the current Three-Self union would break away to establish new denominational structures, churches, and Christian institutions.

To keep from falling apart, the Three-Self union of Protestant churches would have to be reinvented. First, the TSPM would have to shed the ill-fitting attire of political ideology and array itself in the theological and liturgical garments of the church. This process has been going on for some time, but now its urgency would finish the transformation from government organ to true church. The difficult task of reestablishing common ground in Christ and the church, as opposed to political loyalty, would also need to be undertaken. Loss of the government cudgel would require leaders to woo rather than to rule by fiat, but such reform is long overdue. Being forced to attract rather than to command would allow gifted young leadership to rise and remove dead wood moored to government sinecure. In the end, this reform and renewal would revitalize the organization. In addition to their status, connections, resources, established seminaries, and churches, the union would enjoy a distinct advantage over their rivals.

Shedding the ideological cocoon that preserved yet restricted the life and vitality of Christians within the TSPM would allow them to fulfill a destiny too long denied. Leaders of the TSPM have long served as the bridge between the Communist Party and the official Christian community. Familiarity with the desires and fears of both government officials and Christian believers gives leaders of the TSPM precious insight during a time of sweeping change. If the TSPM put this insight to proper use, they could lower anxiety and avert possible conflicts that might arise. In so doing, they could be agents of grace to many who have feared and avoided them as arbiters of injustice.

Theological education, however, is where the TSPM will play its most critical role. Even in a less-restrictive environment, independent churches will lack the resources, talent, and expertise necessary to establish viable seminaries in China. In contrast, the TSPM already operates seminaries in nearly every province in China. Their extensive international connections to seminaries worldwide would enable them to tap the critical resources needed to expand theological education in China. Although most independent churches currently distrust TSPM seminaries, the dire need of sound theological education would persuade some to risk sending their future pastors to be trained there. If the divided church of China is ever to mend, these seminaries will need to provide the space where past wounds can be healed and Christians be reconciled with one another. Even if that did not result in institutional union, it would go far to forging spiritual union between believers.

Wither the Divided Church in China?

Reading the tea leaves of official religious policy of the Chinese government has never been easy. Reports of substantial reform must be tempered with sober recognition of ongoing persecution of house churches. Separate registration may alleviate the risk of government harassment for some, but it could be a ploy to draw some independent groups into the fold while others bear the brunt of brutal suppression.

The seesaw policy of the government over the last fifty years is hardly reassuring. The current leadership's tolerant feelings toward the church today offer no guarantee of what it will do tomorrow. Because policy is rarely carried out uniformly in China, the risks of registration would fall differently in different places. Much would depend on local officials and how they wished to interpret and enforce any new policy that might be handed down.

If true reform arrives, Western nations and Christians will play an important role. Chinese political leaders, it is true, regard Western criticism of Chinese religious policy as an irritant. In light of the humiliating colonial legacy of Western dominance in China, foreign concerns can often be interpreted as lack of respect for China's sovereignty and dignity. That said, China does factor into its foreign policy Western pressure on human-rights issues. Thus, effective diplomacy will require that pressure be applied subtly, so as not to force the Chinese government to defend its honor. Consistency, care, and long-term commitment in relationships are key to influencing policy in China. Those who tend to such matters are granted a hearing, and their views carry weight.

Although carefully worded criticism will at times be required, it must be balanced with appropriate recognition of the ongoing reform process taking place in China. Thus, effective engagement will require political and ecclesial rhetoric to move beyond mere criticism as those concerned help leaders and officials arrive at solutions that will actually work in China. For example, calls for China to adopt unfettered religious liberty stand little chance of being heard. On the other hand, models of religious tolerance in places such as Singapore, which allows churches to govern themselves with a minimum of government requirements, are far more likely to be embraced.

Western Christians need to recognize that both house churches and TSPM churches represent millions of Christians and that acknowledging only one party in this divide merely complicates matters. Too often churches that defend the TSPM ignore or scoff at well-documented instances of brutal persecution. Conversely, some supporters of the house churches treat all TSPM churches as apostate and nothing more than government puppets. Neither of these attitudes is appropriate or helpful. Both groups have pastors, church leaders, and members who are sincere and disciplined Christians. Indeed, though it is right to describe the church in China as divided, that divide represents a spectrum of relative harmony and hostility between the two sides. Only through an appreciation of the complex nature of the churches of China can Western Christians come to understand both the wonder and the predicament in which Chinese Christians and the government find themselves in today.

Regardless of which policy the Chinese government pursues, the church in China will profoundly affect the shape of Christianity worldwide for generations to come. With some thirty to seventy million souls and a growth rate of 7 percent annually,[10] the number of Christians in China dwarfs the number of Christians in most nations of the earth. Like Christians throughout the developing world, Chinese Christians represent the vanguard of the church in the twenty-first century. Their distinct character and virtues in many ways reflect the character and legacy of Wang Mingdao.

Although the church in China has, like Wang, at times stumbled and cracked under pressure, it always seems to return stronger than before. Decades of opposition and suffering have served to discipline the church and enabled it to persevere when others imagined it extinct. Having survived the difficult years, the question remains: Will the church maintain its rigor if the churches are granted autonomy from the state? As history will testify, the church has often fared better in times of suffering and persecution than in times of prosperity and official patronage. When Billy Graham visited Wang Mingdao, Wang told him that he now lived for only one thing: to be faithful unto death. Certainly the concern for Christianity in China will be that it maintain its integrity, perseverance, and faith in times of liberty even as it has in times of suffering.

Like Wang, the church has experienced a remarkable change of fortunes. Weak, despised, and considered a relic of a hated era, the church suffered the wrath of the nation. Buried and left for dead, it has now arisen to capture the heart and mind of millions of Chinese and has become a force to be reckoned with. Having handled humiliation well, how will the church handle its ascendancy? The exhaustion of the Decian persecutions in the fourth century gave birth to the temptation of patronage under Constantine. Certainly Christians today should be wary that their very success could pose a dangerous temptation in a land that has historically fused the Mandate of Heaven with political power. Will humility, suffering, and weakness continue to be embraced in an emerging China enamored with wealth, power, and conspicuous consumption?

The Legacy of Wang Mingdao: What Is in a Name?

Wang preferred to be addressed simply as "Mr. Wang Mingdao." If titles cut against the doctrinal grain of this hardbitten man, how much more would the paeans lifted up in his name? Nevertheless, for Christians throughout China and beyond, Wang's writings, stand, and enduring influence continue to be honored.

Wang Mingdao's works, which fill over seven volumes, are not scholarly tomes. They do not contain theological breakthroughs or fetes of biblical scholarship. His autobiography, commentaries on Scripture, sermons, and essays were forged to lay hold of the conscience of common people and expose evils cleverly wrapped in the pretense of modernist cant. Nonetheless, Wang's works represent a treasury whose value could easily be overlooked. His works continue to be published, read, and applied in Chinese churches across Asia. His direct and simple prose, his clever use of biblical figures, and his piercing dissection of his opponents' arguments continue to inspire and inform Christians in Asia. Moreover, though not scholarly works in themselves, Wang's works provide an invaluable resource for scholars. Unlike most Christian intellectuals and writers of his age, Wang conveyed an understanding of the gospel that resonated throughout the churches of China and beyond. Careful examination of his works provide insight as to why he was able to reach so many when others were so ineffective. The only person of comparable influence was Watchman Nee, but even though Nee's works are interesting, his early imprisonment cut him off from being able to comment on the critical issues we have examined in this book. In years to come, careful examination of the work of Wang Mingdao should provide important insight into the growth and perseverance of the church in China.

The fact that Wang Mingdao was the last pastor standing against the wave that swept up all others in its wake had as much to do with his temperament as with his virtue. Only the most obdurate would resist as long as he did. Yet that doggedness was the knife that ripped open the underbelly of issues too easily ignored and too easily denied by those willing to yield to the prevailing political winds. Had Wang been willing to establish official ties with foreign missionaries, agreed to join a larger denomination, or pacified the Japanese need for control, he could have been swept aside much sooner. Yet his intractability on matters of integrity made him a hard and costly target to take down. Because he was tough he forced those opposed to him to reveal their true hand. His stand forced the TSPM leaders to shed their Christian vestments to reveal their political corset. His stand forced the government to lower the mask of an avowed "freedom of religion" to bare the rigid countenance of doctrinaire Maoist ideology. His stand forced Western scholars to deviate from their defense of a church at home in an avowedly Marxist country to somehow provide divine sanction for the persecution of those who demurred. Truly "a stone of stumbling and a rock of offense," Wang's legacy continues to discomfit all who push up against it.

Wang Mingdao died quietly in his home in Shanghai on July 28, 1991. His wife Jingwen died the following year. The only physical reminder of their presence is a simple stone in Beijing noting their birth and death. Nonetheless, if twenty years of imprisonment and thirty-five years of enforced silence could not erase the memory of Wang Mingdao, how much less the years that have passed since his death. Even were his name to pass from the memory and lips of Christians in China, it would be hard to remove his more important legacy found in the perseverance, tenacity, and faith of the Chinese church. Like Wang Mingdao, though despised, humiliated, and hounded, its pluck in the midst of strife astounds even the most jaded observer. After nearly fifteen hundred years of sporadic and unsuccessful attempts to establish Christianity in China and after a century that found it on the brink of destruction, the church of China has not only survived, but thrived. Given its legacy, the church of China will now endure, built upon the lives and stories of those who persevered.

Servant of God, well done, well hast thou fought
The better fight, who single hast maintaind
Against revolted multitudes the Cause
Of Truth, in word mightier then they in Armes
And for the testimonie of Truth hast born
Universal reproach, far worse to beare
Then violence: for this was all thy care
To stand approv'd in sight of God, though Worlds
Judg'd thee perverse . . .[11]

 APPENDIX 1

The Christian Manifesto

(This key document was written in May 1950, worked out by the founding group of the TSPM in consultation with Premier Zhou Enlai. It was eventually signed by at least 400,000 Protestant Christians in a mass campaign for public endorsement of the document.)

Protestant Christianity has been introduced to China for more than a hundred and forty years. During this period it has made a not unworthy contribution to Chinese society. Nevertheless, and this was most unfortunate, not long after Christianity's coming to China, imperialism started its activities here; and since the principal groups of missionaries who brought Christianity to China all came themselves from these imperialistic countries, Christianity consciously or unconsciously, directly or indirectly, became related with imperialism. Now that the Chinese revolution has achieved victory, these imperialistic countries will not rest passively content in face of this unprecedented historical fact in China. They will certainly seek to contrive by every means the destruction of what has actually been achieved; they may also make use of Christianity to forward their plot of stirring up internal dissension, and creating reactionary forces in this country. It is our purpose in publishing the following statement to heighten our vigilance against imperialism, to make known the clear political stand of Christians in New China, to hasten the building of a Chinese Church whose affairs are managed by the Chinese themselves, and to indicate the responsibilities that should be taken up by Christians throughout the whole country in national reconstruction in New China. We desire to call upon all Christians in the country to exert their best efforts in putting into effect the principles herein presented.

The Task in General

Christian churches and organizations give thoroughgoing support to the "Common Political Platform," and under the leadership of the government oppose imperialism, feudalism, and bureaucratic capitalism, and take part in the effort to build an independent, democratic, peaceable, unified, prosperous, and powerful New China.

Fundamental Aims

Christian churches and organizations in China should exert their utmost efforts, and employ effective methods, to make people in the churches everywhere recognize clearly the evils that have been wrought in China by imperialism; recognize that in the past imperialism has made use of Christianity; purge imperialistic influences from within Christianity itself; and be vigilant against imperialism, and especially American imperialism, in its plot to use religion in fostering the growth of reactionary forces. At the same time, the churches and organizations should call upon Christians to participate in the movement opposing war and upholding peace, and teach them thoroughly to understand and support the government's policy of agrarian reform. Christian churches and organizations in China should take effective measures to cultivate a patriotic and democratic spirit among their adherents in general, as well as a psychology of self-respect and self-reliance. The movement for autonomy, self-support, and self-propagation hitherto promoted in the Chinese Church has already attained a measure of success. This movement from now onwards should complete its tasks within the shortest possible period. At the same time, self-criticism should be advocated, all forms of Christian activity reexamined and readjusted, and thoroughgoing austerity measures adopted, so as to achieve the goals of a reformation in the Church.

Concrete Methods

All Christian churches and organizations in China that are still relying upon foreign personnel and financial aid should work out concrete plans to realize within the shortest possible time their objective of self-reliance and rejuvenation.

From now onwards, as regards their religious work, Christian churches and organizations should lay emphasis upon a deeper understanding of the nature of Christianity itself, closer fellowship and unity among the various denominations, the cultivation of better leadership personnel, and reform in systems of Church organization. As regards their more general work, they should emphasize anti-imperialistic, anti-feudalistic, and anti-bureaucratic-capitalistic education, together with such forms of service to the people as productive labor, teaching them to understand the New Era, cultural and recreational activities, literacy education, medical and public health work, and care of children.

Editor's note: When this Manifesto was published, a covering letter signed by Bishop Kuang, T. C. Chao, Y. T. Wu, Cora Deng, Y. C. Tu, H. H. Tsui, L. M. Liu, and N. S. Ai went out to Chinese Christian leaders, making some of the statements in the Manifesto more explicit. The Church must support the Common Platform, accept the leadership of the Government and work harmoniously with it. It must come to a clear understanding of the way American imperialism has used the Church, and eradicate all the results of that imperialism. As a principle it must use no foreign funds and no foreign personnel, and on these two points it must consult with the Government. During the period of Land Reform all Church activities except routine Sunday services, prayer-meetings, etc., should cease.[1]

Wang Mingdao's "Self-Examination"

I am a counterrevolutionary offender. As a result of the patient attitude shown by the Government and the reeducation given me I have come to realize my errors. I have been accorded generous treatment by the Government and have been saved from the abyss of crime. For this my heart is full of gratitude. When I think of what I did in the past I am deeply distressed and ashamed. Already I have made a frank statement of my offenses to the Government. Today I simply want to talk to you about how I used religious forms to carry on counterrevolutionary activities.

As a citizen of my country I should observe its laws and support all the Government policies and programs. As a preacher I should lead Christian believers along this course. Yet I constantly spread reactionary statements and tried to sabotage various Government plans and the socialist reconstruction movement.

When American imperialists launched the Korean War in 1950, they not only trampled upon the soil and the people of Korea but they also threatened our northeast provinces. If we had not resisted, our country would have encountered unimaginable disaster. After the

"Resist-America Aid-Korea Movement" began, the people of the whole country gave their full strength in support so as to drive back the invaders and defend our native land. Because I had long cherished anti-government and anti-Communist thoughts, I tried to undermine the Resist-America Aid-Korea Movement. I used such quotations as "They that take the sword shall perish with the sword" (Matt. 26:52) to urge Christian believers not to join the army; I said that Christians should not contribute death-dealing weapons to the war effort; I opposed their engaging in military service and giving money to the purchase of airplanes and big guns. After military service law was promulgated, I declared openly in my sermons and Bible classes that Christians should not obey. I used the words of Jesus, "They that take the sword shall perish with the sword" to stop Christians from taking up arms, and in private conversations with Christians I said that they should go to prison rather than become soldiers. As a matter of fact, the Bible tells of Christians who engaged in military service and fought; the centurion Cornelius is an example. The Constitution of our Republic states that all citizens of military age have the duty to be soldiers and to defend their country so that it will not suffer aggression. Yet I sought to sabotage military service.

The "Three-Anti Movement" was a mighty effort to wipe out the graft, the official corruption, the greed, and rottenness of many thousand years. Every citizen should support such a movement. However, I slandered the Movement by saying that it was marked with lies, cruelty, and anti-religious activity. Our national Constitution has a clear statement about religious liberty. The Government has constantly pursued a policy of protecting the freedom of religious belief. Since liberation, our Christian Church has not once been hindered in its work and our religious freedom has not been infringed upon by the Government. Yet, out of hostility to the Government and the Communist Party, I constantly used my sermons, writings, and private conversations with believers, to describe past persecutions suffered by the Church. I made much of these persecutions in history, and falsely accused our Government of religious persecution. I preached and wrote on such topics as: "Does he sit or stand?"; "He who dies daily" (1 Cor. 15:31); "Fear not those who threaten you." I encouraged believers to struggle unto death in opposition to the Government. I told them that in this way they could receive honor and welcome from Christ; even Christ Himself on His throne would stand up to welcome those who sacrificed themselves for His sake. Some believers under my influence carried on anti-government activities. Because of my hostile attitude to the Government and the Communist Party my preaching contained many antagonistic insinuations against the Government and Communist Party.

Using the excuse of theological differences l was always stirring up believers against unbelievers, believers against the Government, and creating opposition. Once I preached a sermon on "Is there any new thing on earth?" in which I quoted the verse from the Bible, "There is no new thing under the sun" (Eccles. 1:9) to say that whatever changes took place on earth men are always sinners before God and therefore cannot accomplish any new thing. I used a troupe of actors as an illustration and said that no matter what play they performed on the stage they were still the same group of actors. In this way I discredited the many new persons and new accomplishments in our modern Chinese society and caused my hearers to belittle the changes and the progress that had taken place and even to deny them. I said that those who do not believe in God are "fools, evil men, devil's people." I said also that such persons are planning to destroy believers in God and to wipe out the Christian Church. All such talk caused believers and unbelievers to stand against each other. Again, I cried out that "believers should not be yoked together with unbelievers" and urged believers to separate themselves from unbelievers. I even preached that Christians are those who break with the crowd; as a result many believers became queer people who could not cooperate with others and who thus failed to make the proper contribution to our nation and society. Actually believers and unbelievers are different only in respect to religious faith and should practice mutual honor. In our opposition to imperialism, in our patriotic activities, in our building of a socialist society, it is imperative that we unite and work together. But in my bigoted statements I strayed far off the path of right relations between believers and unbelievers and made unity and cooperation more difficult, even impossible.

Socialist construction is a great task which all citizens should support and in which all should participate. It is vitally related to the future development and destiny of our country. Nevertheless, I failed to encourage believers to support socialist construction and to take part in it; I even worked hard to sabotage it. Once in a sermon I said, "If death continues on earth, then no matter how much men may improve society it cannot be considered ideal." By ridiculing socialist society I made my audience lose their eagerness for the building of a new society and become unwilling to participate actively in reconstruction. I even built up antagonism to socialist construction. Some believers under my influence opposed the organization in government bureaus and schools and took a stand against the leadership; they did not perform their work well. When the purge of counter-revolutionaries started I should have led my congregation to support this movement; I should have encouraged doubtful persons to make a clean breast of their past. Not only did I fail to do this but I misrepresented the Government by saying it was using the movement to attack Christians; I went so far as to urge Christians to resist. I said, "We must risk everything, ourselves, our families, our lives, our future, for Christ." When a believer once said that he did not answer questions put to him in an indoctrination class I commended his behavior. When another Christian reported to me about his study-group (in Communism) I said to him, "Since the Government wants to attack us, it is useless to talk very much; better not say anything." When Ku Shui-hua testified in our Church meeting how he resisted indoctrination, I urged other believers to imitate his example, to be as firm and brave as he was. In all these ways I sabotaged the movement against counterrevolutionaries. When Hsu Hung-Tao was arrested in Tientsin and his wife and fellow-workers discussed the situation with me, I urged them to raise questions with the Bureau of Public Safety in Tientsin and advised them how to deal with the Government. I gave the suggestions regarding a letter to Government authorities. In all this affair I suspected the Government of attacking religion and persecuting preachers. Moreover, I reported what had happened at a supper in our Church and said that the Government had done wrong, thus causing dissatisfaction among the believers. In all these things

I did not stand on the side of the people but on the side against the people; and many Christians because of me took the same attitude.

From the beginning of the Three-Self Reform Movement in the summer of 1951 I opposed the Movement. I wrongly declared that the Government was using this Movement to destroy the Church. I bitterly attacked the Movement and its leaders, and all the preachers who joined it. I wrote articles criticizing them. I used the fiercest language to accuse them, oppose them, and revile them. In June, 1955, I published an article, *We—For the Sake of Faith* in which I asserted that Fundamentalists and modernists should not cooperate and took my stand against the Three-Self Patriotic Movement, its leaders, and all who worked with them. My article influenced many people and seriously hurt the Three-Self Patriotic Movement.

This Movement is not something in the area of theological doctrine; it is a movement inside the Church for love of country and resistance to imperialism. Since liberation all the people of our nation, of all classes, have eagerly participated in the patriotic and anti-imperialist movement. Christians cannot stand aside from this movement. The Church in China was influenced for a long time by imperialism and many people in it have had connections with imperialism; all the more reason, therefore, why we should promote self-government, self-support, and self-propagation, and push the anti-imperialist movement. Yet I did not join the Movement; I even opposed it and tried to ruin it. I influenced other churches not to join and some, which had joined, to pull out. Using the pretext of theological disagreement I weakened the unity of the Christian Church and the anti-imperialist movement inside the Church. I made an exceedingly grievous mistake. Now I know that imperialist poison has existed within the Church; this has nothing to do with the Bible and biblical doctrine; it does not belong in the Bible. The worship of America and Britain and other such common attitudes are not scriptural at all, yet I formerly objected to those who would rid the Church of such poisons. Now I know that the ejection of these poisons will not injure the Church but will cleanse it and bring benefit to it.

Another matter I must sorrowfully confess. American imperialists at the Geneva Conference in 1954 used my name to create rumors and to slander the Government of China; they said that Wang Ming-dao had been executed. Every Chinese citizen should have been angry at such a report. From the ethical point of view it was falsehood and deceit worthy of severe condemnation. Yet I did not criticize this sin of American imperialists; I just considered myself an object of special attention by the whole world. When in August of that year I read an interview given by Bishop Robin Chen to a correspondent of the Hsin-hua News Agency denying the rumor of my execution and a special news item about me in the *Takungpao* (daily newspaper) in April, 1955, I thought that the Government because of world concern about my safety would hesitate to take any action against me. Thereupon I grew bolder and more reckless in my reactionary activities. The American rumors had the effect of encouraging and strengthening me in my wrong stand; I say it today with shame. This business alone shows how much I lacked in national and racial consciousness. I stood entirely with the imperialists. I can only condemn myself and confess my sin to the Government and the people.

I have committed a serious offense. The reason was not any theological difficulty but simply my hostile point of view toward the Communist Party and the People's Government. My reactionary ideas were a result of years of reactionary propaganda. Since about 1928 I have been reading in reactionary publications vicious propaganda against the Communist Party. With every possible kind of misrepresentation and slander, the writers have pictured the Communist Party as a "raging flood and wild beast." This propaganda penetrated my mind and engendered in me an intense hatred of the Communist Party. Moreover, for many years I was in constant contact with imperialist elements and was corrupted by them. They were always making up falsehoods about the Communist Party, saying that it was cruel, deceitful, antireligious, a persecutor of Christians, and so on. I was deeply affected by this propaganda and developed a hostile attitude to the Communist Party and the People's Government. Even after liberation my reactionary viewpoint did not change; I continued to cherish ideas contradictory to the Communist Party and the People's Government.

I was unwilling to face realities; good achievements of the Government I looked upon as evil; besides, I influenced and corrupted many other people.

I now discern my past faults. I know that as a citizen I should support all the policies and programs of the Government and obey all its laws. As a preacher I should lead all believers to obey the laws and support the Government, to unite with all people in the country for the good of our fatherland. My former antigovernment activities were indeed wrong; they caused harm to the people and produced an evil effect upon many believers. I sincerely repent before the people and the Government, and hope that those who were led astray by me will return to the right road.

Finally, I wish to express my genuine thanks to the Government for the teaching and the help that they have given me. They have enabled me to see all my past errors. Because of the magnanimous treatment which I have received I am determined to lead Christian believers in obeying the laws, in devotedly serving their fatherland, in supporting all Government policies and plans, in joining the great united body within the Christian Church, and in the movement against imperialism. I shall guide the believers in the Church and the people of the nation in tasks of socialist construction. I shall try to win back the good persons whom I led astray and to set them free from the bad influences which I once brought to bear upon them. I shall tell them what I learned in my recent studies. Although I cannot make up for all previous losses, yet I shall do my best to recover lost ground and to become a truly patriotic and society-loving preacher.

I wish also to apologize to the preachers who have joined the Three-Self Patriotic Movement and their leaders. On numerous occasions I attacked them without reason and reviled them; in my sermons and writings I defamed them on the ground that they were helping atheists to destroy the Church. For this I beg everyone's pardon. Moreover, in 1955, I refused to see representatives appointed by the National Christian Conference in Peking to visit me. For this ungrateful act and for any other wrong behavior I ask pardon from all concerned and from my country. For everything in the past I ask everyone's forgiveness.[1]

Notes

Introduction

1. The original quotation used the pinyin romanization "Ding Guangxun." Though in general I will follow the pinyin romanization when transliterating Chinese terminology, with personal names I have put in the form most widely used and recognized by those familiar with these persons. Thus, K. H. Ting, Y. T. Wu, and T. C. Chao are used as opposed to Ding Guangxun, Wu Yaozong, and Zhao Zichen. As for Wang Mingdao and Mao Zedong, these two names now commonly appear in pinyin romanization and thus remain so in this text.

2. Such disparity in determining the size of the church in China results from several factors: (1) the difficulty of determining actual numbers, given the illegal nature of the house churches; and (2) the tendency either to over-report or under-report the size of the church, depending on who is doing the counting. The number attending officially sanctioned churches is currently at around ten million. House-church numbers vary between twenty to fifty million, with a growth rate estimated at around 7 percent annually (Erik Eckholm, "China Charges Eighty-Five in Religion Crackdown," *New York Times*, 6 September 2000).

Chapter 1: What's in a Name?

1. The contemporary significance of what one calls these events was highlighted by the recent (1 October 2000) Vatican decision to canonize 120 Chinese martyrs. The Chinese government, through the state-run press, protested the Vatican decree, stating that the canonization honored "imperialists" who "repressed" the Chinese people and were put to death as a result of the "righteous indignation of the people." In contrast, Pope John Paul II pointed out eighteen-year-old Chi Zhuzi, who announced to his Boxer captors, even as they prepared to skin him alive, that "every piece of my flesh, every drop of my blood will repeat for you that I am a Christian" (reported in "Making Saints," ABC News Internet, 1 October 2000). It is interesting to note that in their excellent history of China, Fairbank and Reischauer describe this same event as "the Boxer Movement," thus emphasizing a directional element rather than characterizing the event as either an unlawful revolt or a righteous reaction (John K. Fairbank and Edwin O. Reischauer,

China: Tradition and Transformation [Boston: Allen & Unwin, 1979]). One senses here the imaginative construct of "nationalism" as the underlying structure used to understand and interpret the event in question. For a better understanding of how nationalism functions as a reductive warrant, see Benedict Anderson, *Imagined Communities: Reflections on the Origin and Spread of Nationalism* (New York: Verso, 1991).

2. Eyewitness account quoted in G. Thompson Brown's *Earthen Vessels and Transcendent Power: American Presbyterians in China, 1837-1952* (Maryknoll, New York: Orbis Books, 1997), 152.

3. Often Chinese will have several names given to them, or taken by them, through life. Wang's pet name was Wang Tie (Iron Wang); later, when he entered primary school, he was given the name Yongsheng (Everlasting Abundance) (Leslie Lyall, *Three of China's Mighty Men* [London: Overseas Missionary Fellowship, 1973], 97–104).

4. Wang Mingdao, *A Stone Made Smooth* (Southhampton, Eng.: Mayflower Christian Books, 1981), 13.

5. Wang Mingdao, *Wu Shi Nian Lai (These Fifty Years)* (Beijing: Spiritual Food Quarterly Special Publications, 1950), 3.

6. Wang, *A Stone Made Smooth*, 16.

7. Ibid.

8. Ibid., 10.

9. Ibid., 23.

10. Wang, *Wu Shi Nian Lai*, 27–28.

11. G. Thompson Brown, *Earthen Vessels and Transcendent Power: American Presbyterians in China, 1837–1952* (Maryknoll, N.Y.: Orbis, 1997), 154.

12. Wang, *Wu Shi Nian Lai*, 46–47. Wang's pacifism and opposition to military training at the Presbyterian school at Baoding is not included in either Arthur Reynolds's abridged version of *Wu Shi Nian Lai, A Stone Made Smooth*, or Leslie Lyall's *Three of China's Mighty Men*, which tells the story of Wang Mingdao's life and eventual conflict with officials in China. Wang's pacifism was a major point of

contention between Wang and conservative missionaries in China, who agreed with his conservative evangelical doctrine but rejected his pacific tendencies. Wang's autobiography, *Wu Shi Nian Lai*, was written in 1950, before the conflict with the Three-Self Patriotic Movement erupted. Lyall's *Three of China's Mighty Men* was written after Wang's arrest and imprisonment. All of this reveals a fundamental and critical difference between the position of Wang Mingdao and his evangelical defenders. Whereas Wang Mingdao's pacifism and resistance arose in light of the issues of modernism and nationalism, it is interpreted by his defenders as fundamentally anti-communist.

13. Wang, *A Stone Made Smooth*, 49.

14. Ibid., 56.

15. Ibid., 65–66.

16. Ibid., 71.

17. Ibid., 74.

18. Francis P. Jones, *The Church in Communist China: A Protestant Appraisal* (New York: Friendship Press, 1962), 103.

19. Wang, *A Stone Made Smooth*, 165.

20. Ibid., 201.

Chapter 2: A Church Divided: Modernism, Fundamentalism, and the Anti-Christian Movement

1. According to Yip Ka-che, *Religion, Nationalism and Chinese Students: The Anti-Christian Movement of 1922–1927* (Bellingham, Wash.: Center for East Asian Studies, Western Washington University, 1980), this movement effectively ended the possibility of China adopting Christianity as the religious subtext for social and national development in China.

2. Jonathan Chao, "The Chinese Indigenous Church Movement, 1919–1927: A Protestant Response to the Anti-Christian Movements in Modern China" (Ph.D. diss., University of Pennsylvania, 1986).

3. Chu Sin-Jan, *Wu Leichuan: A Confucian-Christian in Republican China* (New York: Peter Lang, 1995), 33.

4. Ng Lee-ming, "Christianity and Social Change: The Case in China, 1920–1950" (Diss., Princeton Theological Seminary, 1970), 109.

5. T. C. Chao, "Can Christianity Be the Basis of Social Reconstruction in China?" quoted in Ng, "Christianity and Social Change," 112–13.

6. Ng, "Christianity and Social Change," 191.

7. Ibid., 175–76.

8. Ibid., 180.

9. Y. T. Wu, "Revolution and Student Thought," quoted in ibid., 199.

10. Ng, "Christianity and Social Change," 204–26.

11. Y. T. Wu, "The Present Day Tragedy of Christianity," in *Documents of the Three-Self Movement: Source Materials for the Study of the Protestant Church in Communist China*, ed. F. P. Jones (New York: National Council of the Churches of Christ, 1963), 1–5.

12. Y. T. Wu, "On Reforming Christianity" (1949), in *Documents of the Three-Self Movement*, 14.

13. Wang Mingdao was a tireless preacher, writer, and evangelist. A treasury of his sermons and writings, which ended upon his imprisonment at age fifty-five, has been combined into seven volumes, which do not include his autobiography written in 1950. See *Wang Ming Dao Wen Ke (Treasuries of Wang Ming Dao)*, ed. C. C. Wang, 7 vols. (Taichung, Taiwan: Conservative Baptist Press, 1996).

14. Wang Mingdao, *Spiritual Food*, trans. Arthur Reynolds (Southhampton, Eng.: Mayflower Christian Books, 1983), 23.

15. Ibid., 121.

16. Ibid., 125.

17. Ibid., 81–82.

18. Ibid., 84.

19. Ng, "Christianity and Social Change," 83.

20. Wang, *Spiritual Food*, 84.

21. Wang, *A Stone Made Smooth*, 140–41.

22. Wang, *Spiritual Food*, 44.

23. Ibid., 95.

24. Ibid., 121.

25. Ibid., 124.

26. Wang, *Spiritual Food*, 128.

27. Wang began printing *Spiritual Food Quarterly* in spring 1927. It ran for twenty-five years and ended with his imprisonment. He set aside periods each year to write and publish this journal. Nearly thirty books were produced from these writings, which included his sermons, Scripture expositions, and editorials (cf. Lyall, *Three of China's Mighty Men*, 112–13.).

28. Perhaps the most prolific Chinese Christian writer to date, Wang wrote so extensively that his compiled works, excluding his biographical books, make up a seven-volume compendium that continues to be published in Taiwan and to be read by Chinese Christians around the world. Wang's last forty years are recorded in *You Si Shi Nian (The Last Forty Years)* published posthumously from material he recorded secretly and had carried out of China during his last years in Shanghai.

29. Though Wang Mingdao provided hard numbers in regards to seating capacity at the various houses where his church worshiped, he neglects to give the exact seating capacity for the Christian Tabernacle that they had built. He records that 500 people attended the opening service, but at the service in 1955 on the day of his arrest he states that between 700 and 800 worshipers attended service that morning. Unless the building was expanded I can only surmise that it could seat 800 persons. Wang, *A Stone Made Smooth*, 115–22. Stephen C. H. Wang, *Wang Ming Dao: You Si Shi Nian (The Last Forty Years)* (Scarbourough, Ont.: Canada Gospel Publishing House, 1997), 98. The material for this book was drawn from recordings made by Wang Mingdao in Shanghai not long before his death. The recordings were then taken out of the country and published posthumously. This work details previously unknown details of Wang's arrest and imprisonment. All quotes from this book are my translation.

30. Wang, *A Stone Made Smooth*, 123.

31. Ibid., 124ff.

32. Ibid., 129–30.

33. Wang, *Wu Shi Nian Lai* (my translation) 179.

34. Wang, *A Stone Made Smooth*, 140–41.

35. Ibid., 224.

36. Ibid., 210.

37. Ibid., 230.

38. Ibid., 236.

Chapter 3: Joining the United Front: The Church and the Chinese Communist Party

1. Quoted in Donald E. MacInnis, *Religious Policy and Practice in Communist China: A Documentary History* (New York: MacMillan, 1972), 12.

2. "New China" *(Xin Hua)* was a term coined in Chinese to represent China after the revolution.

3. Statement of Emperor Pu Yi, as quoted in Fairbank and Reischauer, *China: Tradition and Transformation*, 415.

4. Mao Zedong, "On the People's Democratic Dictatorship" (1949), in *Selected Works of Mao Tse-tung*, 5 vols. (Peking: Foreign Languages Press, 1965), 4:422.

5. Mao Zedong, "Don't Hit Out in All Directions" (1950), in *Selected Works of Mao Tse-tung*, 5 vols. (Peking: Foreign Languages Press, 1965), 5:33–34.

6. Inner-Party directive issued 25 December 1940, quoted in Lyman P. Van Slyke, *Enemies and Friends: The United-Front in Chinese Communist History* (Stanford, Calif.: Stanford University Press, 1967), 271.

7. Van Slyke, *Enemies and Friends*, 100–1.

8. Mao Zedong, "On the Correct Handling of Contradictions among the People" (1957), in *Selected Works of Mao Tse-tung*, 5 vols. (Peking: Foreign Languages Press, 1965), 5:389.

9. Van Slyke, *Enemies and Friends*, 257.

10. Chen Han-po (1951), quoted in ibid., 216.

11. Yu Ting-ying, "Strengthen Political Thought Education towards Adolescents" (1963), quoted in Bob Whyte, *Unfinished Encounter: China and Christianity* (Glasgow: Collins, 1988), 212.

12. David H. Adeney, *China: Christian Students Face the Revolution* (Downers Grove, Ill.: InterVarsity Press, 1973).

13. This can be particularly seen in the writings of Y. T. Wu, "On Reforming Christianity."

14. The term "Christian Movement" appears to be a name coined by David Paton, a missionary in China, which he gave to a group of young Christian activists who were committed to making Christianity "socially effective." They were deeply influenced by thinkers such as Walter Rauschenbusch and saw in the Social Gospel their own yearnings for national salvation. Most of these leaders were found in the YMCA and YWCA and would form the initial leadership of the fledgling Three-Self Patriotic Movement. See Philip Lauri Wickeri, *Seeking the Common Ground: Protestant Christianity, the Three-Self Movement and China's United Front* (Maryknoll, N.Y.: Orbis, 1988), 125–26; and Whyte, *Unfinished Encounter*, 214–15.

15. Wickeri, *Seeking the Common Ground*, 127.

16. Jones, *The Church in Communist China*, 108.

17. Leslie Lyall, *Come Wind, Come Weather: The Present Experience of the Church in China* (Chicago: Moody Press, 1960), 45–46.

18. Luke Pei-Yuan Lu, "Watchman Nee's Doctrine of the Church with Special Reference to Its Contribution to the Local Church Movement" (Diss., Westminster Theological Seminary, 1992), 1.

19. Ibid., pp. 150–53; see also Angus Kinnear, *The Story of Watchman Nee: Against the Tide* (Wheaton, Ill.: Tyndale House, 1973), 263–69.

20. Church leaders in Shanghai sharply criticized the initial draft that had been sent out, so it was modified. After these modifications were made, it was brought back to receive Zhou Enlai's approval. Although misgivings remained, Y. T. Wu refused to make any further changes (Wickeri, *Seeking the Common Ground*, 129).

21. Gao Wangzhi, "Y. T. Wu: A Christian Leader under Communism," in *Christianity in China from the Eighteenth Century to the Present*, ed. Daniel H. Bays (Stanford, Calif.: Stanford University Press, 1996), 344.

22. "Christian Manifesto," in *Documents of the Three-Self Movement*, 19.

23. Ibid. (my italics).

24. Wickeri, Seeking the Common Ground, 32–42; Whyte, *Unfinished Encounter*, 219–28.

25. The information given here is drawn from *Religion under Socialism in China*, ed. Luo Zhufeng, trans. Donald E. MacInnis and Zheng Xi'an (Armonk, N.Y.: M. E. Sharpe, 1991), 60. This book is actually a report that was written by a group of scholars at the Institute for Research on Religion of the Shanghai Academy of Social Sciences. The names of the writers, editors, and researchers are simply listed at the end of the entire volume with no reference as to which individuals did what or who should be attributed as authors for individual sections. Thus, for references drawn from this work I have simply listed them under *Religion under Socialism in China* and given the appropriate page number.

26. Ibid., 63.

27. Wu, "The Present Day Tragedy of Christianity," 3.

28. Wu, "On Reforming Christianity," 14.

29. Gao, "Y. T. Wu," 351.

30. *Religion under Socialism in China*, 57.

31. Ibid., 58.

32. "Advice on Accusation," in *Documents of the Three-Self Movement*, 49–51.

33. Ibid.

34. This is the self-criticism given by a Christian during the denunciation movement,

"Some of My Experiences and Understanding about Denunciation," originally in the journal *Tian Feng* (1951), quoted in Wickeri, *Seeking the Common Ground*, 136.

35. *Religion under Socialism in China*, 77 (my italics).

36. James Chieh Hsiung, *Ideology and Practice: The Evolution of Chinese Communism* (New York: Praeger, 1970), 154.

37. Wickeri, *Seeking the Common Ground*, 139.

38. *Tian Feng* (1954), quoted in Whyte, *Unfinished Encounter*, 233.

39. Wang Mingdao, "Self-Examination," in *Documents of the Three-Self Movement*, 121.

Chapter 4: Strange News: The Nation As Gospel

1. Merle Goldman, *Literary Dissent in Communist China* (Cambridge, Mass.: Harvard University Press, 1967), 131.

2. Ibid., 143.

3. There are strong indications that Mao himself was deeply involved with the anti–Hu Feng movement (ibid., 149).

4. *Jian Guo Chu Qi Tian-Zhu Jiao, Du Su Jiao Cai Zhong Guo Da Lu: Can Kao Zi Liao* (Bibliographic References Concerning Roman Catholic & Protestant Christianity in Mainland During the Period of National Reconstruction), 3 vols. (Delmar, Calif.: Chinese Research Books, 1995), 3:531. This reference is a collection of documents dealing with religion during the initial years of the establishment of the People's Republic of China. The work includes internal Party documents but consists, for the most part, of a collection of various newspaper articles, of which only some give the author's name and the date of the article. Given the content, the collection period, and the dates on some articles, it is pretty easy to establish that all the articles quoted here were written between 1954 and 1956. From this point on, I will refer to these

documents as *Jian Guo*. All quotations are my own translation.

5. Goldman, *Literary Dissent*, 157.

6. Lyall, *Three of China's Mighty Men*, 131.

7. Ibid.

8. Ibid.

9. Ibid.

10. Wang Mingdao, "Preparation for Suffering," in *A Call to the Church from Wang Ming Dao*, ed. Leona F. Choy, trans. Theodore Choy (Fort Washington, Pa.: Christian Literature Crusade, 1983), 27–28.

11. Wang, "The Missing Voice," in ibid., 35.

12. Ibid., 41–42.

13. Wang, "An Imported Prophet Fails," in ibid., 150.

14. Wang, "Why Fear Threats," ibid., 126.

15. Ibid., 125.

16. Wang, "Preparation for Suffering," 30.

17. K. H. Ting, "Zheng Gao Wang Mingdao" ("A Stern Warning to Wang Mingdao"), *Tian Feng* 477–78 (August 8, 1955), 604 (my translation).

18. *Jian Guo*, 532.

19. Ibid.

20. Ting, "Zheng Gao Wang Mingdao," 608 (my translation).

21. Wang Mingdao, "Zheuli ne? Dusu ne? (Truth or Poison?)" in *Wang Mingdao Wenke* (*Treasuries of Wang Mingdao*), ed. C.C. Wang, pp. 264–65 (my translation).

22. Ibid., 265 (my translation).

23. Ibid., 266 (my translation).

24. Ibid., 268.

25. Ibid., 268ff.

26. Ibid., 275 (my translation).

27. Ibid., 280–81 (my translation).

28. Study Committee Report, "Shengjing Zhenli He Diguo Zhuyi Sixiang Juedui Bu Neng Tiaohe" ("Biblical Truth and Imperialist Poisonous Thought Are Absolutely Incompatible"), *Jin Ling Xie He Xue Yuan Zhi* (*Nanjing Theological Review*) 4 (November 1955): 29–37 (my translation).

29. Ibid., 31.

30. Ibid., 30 (my translation).

31. Ibid., 31 (my translation).

32. Ibid., 34 (my translation).

33. Wang Mingdao, "We Because of Faith," in *Documents of the Three-Self Movement*, 102.

34. Ibid., 104.

35. K. H. Ting, quoted in ibid., 106.

36. Wang, "We Because of Faith," 110–11.

37. Ibid., 111.

38. Ibid., 113–14.

39. Y. T. Wu, "The Future of Christianity in China," in *Documents of the Three-Self Movement*, 175–76.

40. Wickeri, *Seeking the Common Ground*, 219.

Chapter 5: Dividing the Nation— The Arrest and Confession of Wang Mingdao

1. Wang Mingdao, "Self Examination," 117.

2. Stephen C. H. Wang, 98.

3. Ibid., 100.

4. Ibid., 102.

5. The actual confession contained twelve items, but I have combined several that were nearly synonymous.

6. Stephen C. H. Wang, *Wang Ming Dao*, 150.

7. Ibid.

8. Wang's wife was also incarcerated for the same period and separated from Wang up to August 1956, when they were allowed a short visit after Wang had fully confessed and agreed to join the TSPM.

9. Stephen C. H. Wang, *Wang Ming Dao*, 168.

10. Wickeri, *Seeking the Common Ground*, 219.

11. "Unification of Worship" (1958), in *Documents of the Three-Self Movement*, 180.

12. Wang, "Self-Examination," 118–19.

13. Wang himself confessed a lack of "national and *racial* consciousness." The term *minzu* ("racial") could either refer to Chinese ethnic identity (the Han) or represent the

fusion of ethnic identity with citizenship in the new nation. The latter is more likely the case, though appeals to Han solidarity were tied to nationalism throughout the twentieth century and continue to be an important element in China's self-perception and in issues that arise in the relationship between Han and other minority groups (see Prasenjit Duara, *Rescuing History from the Nation: Questioning Narratives of Modern China* [Chicago: University of Chicago Press, 1995], 140–42). What is more important, however, is that regardless of whether or not Wang's reference was to Han identity or national identity, Wang's insistence on a Christian identity based on Scripture and doctrine that preceded the claims of the state divided the people into their religious particularity and thus put him at odds with nationalist views of what constituted *the people*.

14. Wang, "Self-Examination," 120.

15. Vaclav Havel, *Living in Truth*, trans. Jan Vladislav (London: Faber & Faber, 1986), 45.

16. Wang, "Self-Criticism," 121.

17. *Tian Feng* editorial following Wang Mingdao's self-criticism, as translated in Lyall, *Come Wind, Come Weather*, 64–65.

Chapter 6: Underwriting Persecution

1. Ng, "Christianity and Social Change," 94.

2. Leslie Lyall, *Red Sky at Night: Communism Confronts Christianity in China* (London: Hodder & Stoughton, 1969), 115–16.

3. Adeney, *China*, 21.

4. Lyall, *Come Wind, Come Weather*, 33.

5. Lyall, *Three of China's Mighty Men*, 129.

6. Ibid., 51.

7. David M. Paton, *Christian Missions and the Judgment of God* (London: SCM, 1953), 18–19.

8. Ibid., 18.

9. Wing-hung Lam, *Chinese Theology in Construction* (Pasadena, Calif.: William Carey Library, 1983), 78

10. Ibid.

11. Ibid.

12. H. Richard Niebuhr, *Christ and Culture* (New York: Harper & Row, 1951), 80.

13. Ng Lee-ming, "Wang Ming-Tao: An Evaluation of His Thought and Action," *Cheng Feng* 16 (1973): 78 (my italics).

14. Jones, *The Church in Communist China*, 112.

15. Ibid., 114.

16. "A Modus Vivendi" is the title of chapter 6 in Jones's *The Church in Communist China*, 97–114. In this chapter Jones defines the nature of the church's existence in the People's Republic of China.

17. Stephen C. H. Wang, *Wang Ming Dao*, 234.

18. The most explicit example of this was Brother David's *Walking the Hard Road: The Wang Ming-Tao Story* (London: Marshall Pickering, 1989), which is based on interviews Brother David had with Wang Mingdao in Shanghai after his release. Brother David's group was involved in smuggling Bibles into China.

19. Wickeri, *Seeking the Common Ground*, 244–45.

20. Ibid., 157–70.

21. Ibid., 170–85.

22. Ibid., 154.

23. Ibid., 146–57.

24. Ibid., 164.

25. Ibid., 165.

26. Ibid., 166.

27. Ibid., 167–68.

28. Ibid.

Chapter 7: Christian Suffering

1. As quoted in Ivo Lesbaupin, *Blessed Are the Persecuted: Christian Life in the Roman Empire, A.D. 64–313*, trans. Robert Barr (Maryknoll, N.Y.: Orbis, 1987), 50–51.

2. The current relevance of these issues was evident recently in the *New York Times*, as A. M. Rosenthal, columnist for the *Times*, and Van Harvey, professor emeritus at Stanford University, crossed intellectual swords over the issue of the persecution of Chinese Christians (see *International Herald Tribune*, 21 May 1997, 10). In terms of international affairs, shortly before Jiang Zemin's visit to the United States in October 1997, the Chinese government issued an extensive defense of its religious policy, refuting "overseas charges of rigid religious control." The article was particularly noteworthy for its parallels to rhetoric of the 1950s in the denouncement of " 'pernicious' groups which hid behind the *cloak of religion* to *destabilize* the state and conduct illegal activities" (AFP Reuters, *The Straits Times* (Singapore), 17 October 1997, 28 [my italics]).

3. The rise of modern nationalism as the symbolic and narrative structure of modern human existence as well as the reasons for the success of its rather sterile and "shrunken imaginings" is described in Anderson, *Imagined Communities*.

4. Arif Dirlik, *Anarchism in the Chinese Revolution* (Berkeley and Los Angeles: University of California Press, 1991), 51.

5. Duara, 95.

6. Wang, "Self Examination," 120.

7. Ng, "Wang," 78.

8. George M. Marsden, *Fundamentalism and American Culture: The Shaping of Twentieth-Century Evangelicalism 1870–1925* (Oxford: Oxford University Press, 1980), 176.

9. J. I. Packer, *Fundamentalism and the Word of God* (Grand Rapids: Eerdmans, 1958), 73.

10. Marsden, *Fundamentalism*, 146.

11. This is Michael Hollerich's description of Harnack's classical statement of liberal Christianity put forward in *The Essence of Christianity* (1900); cf. Michael Hollerich, "Retrieving a Neglected Critique of Church Theology and Secularization in Weimar Germany," *Pro Ecclesia* 2 (Summer 1993): 312.

12. Paul Althaus, "The Third Reich and the Kingdom of God" (1933), quoted in Klaus Scholder, *The Churches and the Third Reich*, 2 vols. (London: SCM, 1988), 1:104.

13. Emanuel Hirsch, quoted in ibid., 1:106.

14. Karl Barth, *The German Church Conflict* (Richmond, Va.: John Knox, 1965), 44.

15. Hirsch, quoted in Scholder, *The Churches and the Third Reich*, 1:116.

16. See the discussion of "The Present Day Tragedy of Christianity" in chapter 2 above.

17. Hirsch, quoted in Scholder, *The Churches and the Third Reich*, 1:116–17.

18. Karl Barth, *The Doctrine of Creation: The Command of God the Creator*, vol. 3, pt. 4 of *Church Dogmatics*, ed. G. W. Bromiley and T. F. Torrance (Edinburgh: T & T Clark, 1961), 305.

19. Lam, *Chinese*, 78.

20. Barth, *The Doctrine of Creation*, 305.

21. Wickeri, *Seeking the Common Ground*, 166.

22. "The Theological Declaration of Barmen," in *The Book of Confessions: Presbyterian Church USA* (Louisville: Office of the General Assembly PCUSA, 1994), 255–57.

23. Ibid., 257.

24. Barth, *The German Church Conflict*, 44.

25. William James, *The Varieties of Religious Experience* (London: Longmans, Green & Co., 1915), 31.

26. Wang, "Truth or Poison?" 280–81.

27. *Religion under Socialism in China*, 84.

28. Marshall Berman, quoted in Bruce B. Lawrence, *Defenders of God: The Fundamentalist Revolt against the Modern Age* (Columbia: University of South Carolina Press, 1995), 2.

29. Wu, "The Present Day Tragedy," 4 (my italics). Elsewhere in this essay Wu argues that God's will is revealed in the revolutionary movement of his day. Note particularly the resonance between the political theology that underwrites Wu's passage and Althaus's position as well as the nearly identical theological/historical judgment of Ng Lee-ming.

30. Whyte, *Unfinished Encounter*, 244.

31. Lesbaupin, *Blessed Are the Persecuted*, 1–14.

32. Nina Shea, "Atrocities Not Fit to Print," *First Things* 77 (November 1997): 33.

Conclusion: Defying Heaven's Mandate: Wang Mingdao and the Divided Church of China

1. C. K. Yang, *Religion in Chinese Society* (Berkeley: University of California Press, 1961), 127–30.

2. Both Buddhism and Daoism incurred the wrath of the emperor at various times in Chinese history when their size, power, and influence represented a threat to the ritual, spiritual, and political authority of the state. See H. G. Creel, *Chinese Thought from Confucius to Mao Tse-Tung* (New York: Mentor, 1953), 159.

3. Kim-Kwong Chan, "A Chinese Perspective on the Interpretation of the Chinese Government's Religious Policy," in *All under Heaven: Chinese Tradition and Christian Life in the People's Republic of China*, ed. Alan Hunter and Donald Rimmington (Kampen: Kok, 1992), 38–44.

4. Erik Eckholm, "China's Inner Circle Reveals Big Unrest," *New York Times* Internet edition, 3 June 2001.

5. "Seething Mass Anger in China, Insiders Warn," *Straits Times*, 4 June 2001, A3.

6. *International Religious Freedom Report* (Bureau of Democracy, Human Rights, and Labor: U.S. Department of State), 27 October 2001.

7. Staff, BPNews.Net, "2 Christians Killed, Others Tortured in Chinese Government Crackdown" *BP News* Internet edition, 14 January 2002.

8. David Murphy, "Mass Appeal," *Far Eastern Economic Review* Internet edition, 27 December 2001.

9. Ibid.

10. This rate of growth was given in the *Christianity Today* editorial, "Free China's Church" *Christianity Today* Internet edition, 7 January 2002.

11. John Milton, *Paradise Lost*. Great Book Series, vol. 29 (Chicago: Encyclopaedia Britannica, Inc), 197.

Appendix 1: The Christian Manifesto

1. "The Christian Manifesto," in *Documents of the Three-Self Movement: Source Materials for the Study of the Protestant Church in Communist China*, ed. F. P. Jones (New York: National Council of the Churches of Christ, 1963), 19–20.

Appendix 2: Wang Mingdao's "Self-Examination"

1. Wang Mingdao, "Self-Examination," in *Documents of the Three-Self Movement: Source Materials for the Study of the Protestant Church in Communist China*, ed. F. P. Jones (New York: National Council of the Churches of Christ, 1963), 117–21.

Bibliography

Adeney, David H. *China: Christian Students Face the Revolution*. Downers Grove, Ill: InterVarsity Press, 1973.

———. *China: The Church's Long March*. Ventura, Calif.: Regal, 1985.

Anderson, Benedict. *Imagined Communities: Reflections on the Origin and Spread of Nationalism*. New York: Verso, 1991.

Bays, Daniel H. "Christian Revival in China, 1900–1937." In *Modern Christian Revivals*, edited by Edith L. Blumhofer and Randall Balmer, 161–79. Urbana: University of Illinois Press, 1993.

———. "The Growth of Independent Christianity." In *Christianity in China from the Eighteenth Century to the Present*, edited by Daniel H. Bays, 307–16. Stanford, Calif.: Stanford University Press, 1996.

Bohr, Paul Richard. *Religion in the People's Republic of China*. Washington, D.C.: China Council of Asia Society, 1982.

Brook, Timothy. "Toward Independence: Christianity in China under Japanese Occupation, 1937–1945." In *Christianity in China from the Eighteenth Century to the Present*, edited by Daniel H. Bays, 317–36. Stanford, Calif.: Stanford University Press, 1996.

Brown, G. Thompson. *Christianity in the People's Republic of China*. Atlanta: John Knox, 1986.

———. *Earthen Vessels and Transcendent Power: American Presbyterians in China, 1837–1952*. Maryknoll, N.Y.: Orbis, 1997.

Chan, Kim-Kwong. "A Chinese Perspective on the Interpretation of the Chinese Government's Religious Policy." In *All under Heaven: Chinese Tradition and Christian Life in the People's Republic of China*, edited by Alan Hunter and Donald Rimmington, 38–44. Kampen: Kok, 1992.

Chang Hao, *Chinese Intellectuals in Crisis: Search for Order and Meaning*. Berkeley and Los Angeles: University of California Press, 1987.

Chao, Jonathan. "The Chinese Indigenous Church Movement, 1919–1927: A Protestant Response to the Anti-Christian Movements in Modern China." Ph.D. diss., University of Pennsylvania, 1986.

Chu Sin-Jan, *Wu Leichuan: A Confucian-Christian in Republican China*. New York: Peter Lang, 1995.

Cook, Richard R. "A Chinese Fundamentalist: An Examination of the Interaction between the Life and Teaching of Wang

Mingdao and the May Fourth Intellectual Discourse." Unpublished essay.

———. "Fundamentalists in China, 1919–1937: The Pivotal Role of the Bible Union of China As a Link between Nineteenth Century and Late Twentieth Century Missions." Unpublished essay.

Covell, Ralph R. *Confucius, the Buddha, and Christ*. Maryknoll, N.Y.: Orbis, 1986.

Creel, H. G. *Chinese Thought from Confucius to Mao Tse-Tung*. New York: Mentor, 1953.

David, Brother. *Walking the Hard Road: The Wang Ming-Tao Story*. London: Marshall Pickering, 1989.

Derrida, Jacques. *Dissemination*. Translated by Barbara Johnson. Chicago: University of Chicago Press, 1981.

Dirlik, Arif. *Anarchism in the Chinese Revolution*. Berkeley and Los Angeles: University of California Press, 1991.

———. "Modernism and Anti-modernism in Mao Zedong's Marxism." Unpublished essay, Duke University, 1993.

Duara, Prasenjit. "Deconstructing the Chinese Nation." In *Chinese Nationalism*, edited by Jonathan Unger, 31–55. Armonk, N.Y.: M. E Sharpe, 1996.

———. *Rescuing History from the Nation: Questioning Narratives of Modern China*. Chicago: University of Chicago Press, 1995.

Eckholm, Erik. "China Charges Eighty-Five in Religion Crackdown." *New York Times*, 6 September 2000.

Eddy, Sherwood. *Eighty Adventurous Years: An Autobiography*. New York: Harper & Brothers, 1955.

Fairbank, John K., and Edwin O. Reischauer. *China: Tradition and Transformation*. Boston: Allen & Unwin, 1979.

Gao Wangzhi. "Y. T. Wu: A Christian Leader under Communism." In *Christianity in China from the Eighteenth Century to the Present*, edited by Daniel H. Bays, 338–52. Stanford, Calif.: Stanford University Press, 1996.

Giddens, Anthony. *The Nation-State and Violence*. Vol. 2 of *A Contemporary Critique of Historical Materialism*. Berkeley and Los Angeles: University of California Press, 1987.

Goldman, Merle, *Literary Dissent in Communist China*. Cambridge: Harvard University Press, 1967.

Grenz, Stanley J., and Roger E. Olson. *Twentieth Century Theology: God and the World in a Transitional Age*. Downers Grove, Ill.: InterVarsity Press, 1992.

Harvey, Van A. *The Historian and the Believer: The Morality of Historical Knowledge and Belief*. Philadelphia: Westminster, 1966.

Hauerwas, Stanley M. *Christian Existence Today: Essays on Church, World and Living in Between*. Grand Rapids: Brazos Press, 2001.

———. *Dispatches from the Front: Theological Engagements with the Secular*. Durham, N.C.: Duke University Press, 1995.

———. *The Peaceable Kingdom: A Primer in Christian Ethics*. Notre Dame, Ind.: University of Notre Dame Press, 1983.

———. *Vision and Virtue: Essays in Christian Ethical Reflection*. Notre Dame, Ind.: University of Notre Dame Press, 1981.

Havel, Vaclav. *Living in Truth*. Translated by Jan Vladislav. London: Faber & Faber, 1986.

Hobsbawm, E. J. *Nations and Nationalism since 1780: Programme, Myth, Reality*. Cambridge: Cambridge University Press, 1990.

Hollerich, Michael. "Retrieving a Neglected Critique of Church Theology and Secularization in Weimar Germany." *Pro Ecclesia* 2 (Summer 1993): 305–32.

Hood, George. *Neither Bang Nor Whimper: The End of a Missionary Era in China*. Singapore: Presbyterian Church in Singapore, 1991.

Hsiung, James Chieh. *Ideology and Practice: The Evolution of Chinese Communism*. New York: Praeger, 1970.

Hung, William, ed. *As It Looks to Young China*. New York, Friendship Press, 1932.

Hunter, Alan, and Kim-Kwong Chan. *Protestantism in Contemporary China*. Cambridge: Cambridge University Press, 1993.

Hunter, Alan, and Donald Rimmington. *All under Heaven: Chinese Tradition and Christian Life in the People's Republic of China*. Kampen: Kok, 1992.

James, William. *The Varieties of Religious Experience*. London: Longmans, Green & Co., 1915.

Jian Guo Chu Qi Tian-Zhu Jiao, Du Su Jiao Cai Zhong Guo Da Lu: Can Kao Zi Liao. (Bibliographic References Concerning Roman Catholic & Protestant Christianity in Mainland During the Period of National Reconstruction). 3 vols. Delmar, Calif.: Chinese Research Books, 1995.

Jones, Francis P. *The Church in Communist China: A Protestant Appraisal*. New York: Friendship Press, 1962.

———, ed. *China Bulletin* 5/19 (7 November 1955).

———, ed. *Documents of the Three-Self Movement: Source Materials for the Study of the Protestant Church in Communist China*. New York: Far Eastern Office, Division of Foreign Missions National Council of the Churches of Christ in the USA, 1963.

Kauffman, Paul E. *China the Emerging Challenge: A Christian Perspective*. Grand Rapids: Baker, 1982.

Kenneson, Philip D. "There's No Such Thing As Objective Truth and It's a Good Thing, Too." In *Christian Apologetics in the Modern World*, edited by Timothy R. Phillips and Dennis L. Okholm, 155–70. Downers Grove, Ill.: InterVarsity Press, 1995.

Kinnear, Angus. *The Story of Watchman Nee: Against the Tide*. Wheaton, Ill.: Tyndale House, 1973.

Lam, Wing-hung. *Chinese Theology in Construction*. Pasadena, Calif.: William Carey Library, 1983.

———. "The Emergence of Protestant Christian Apologetics in the Chinese Church during the Anti-Christian Movement in the 1920's." Dissertation, Princeton Theological Seminary, 1978.

———. *Wang Ming Dao yu Zhong Guo Jiao Hui* (*Wang Mingdao and the Chinese Church*). Hong Kong: China Graduate School of Theology, 1982.

Lambert, Tony. *The Resurrection of the Chinese Church*. Wheaton, Ill.: Harold Shaw, 1994.

Latourette, Kenneth Scott. *A History of Christian Missions in China*. New York: MacMillan, 1929.

———. *World Service: A History of the Foreign Work and World Service of the Young Men's Christian Associations of the United States and Canada*. New York: Association Press, 1957.

Lawrence, Bruce B. *Defenders of God: The Fundamentalist Revolt against the Modern Age*. Columbia: University of South Carolina Press, 1995.

Lee, Chun Kwan. "The Theology of Revival in the Chinese Christian Church, 1900–1949: Its Emergence and Impact." Diss., Westminster Theological Seminary, 1988.

Lee, Ken Ang. "Watchman Nee: A Study of His Major Theological Themes." Diss., Westminster Theological Seminary, 1989.

Lesbaupin, Ivo. *Blessed Are the Persecuted: Christian Life in the Roman Empire, A.D. 64–313*. Maryknoll, N.Y.: Orbis, 1987.

Levenson, Joseph R. *Confucian China and Its Modern Fate*. 3 vols. Berkeley and Los Angeles: University of California Press, 1968.

Liu Peng. "Church and State Relations in China: Characteristics and Trends." In *Church and State Relations in Twenty-First Century Asia*, edited by Beatrice Leung, 41–55. Hong Kong: Centre of Asian Studies, University of Hong Kong, 1996.

Lu, Luke Pei-Yuan. "Watchman Nee's Doctrine of the Church with Special Reference to Its Contribution to the Local Church Movement." Diss., Westminster Theological Seminary, 1986.

Luo Zhufeng, ed. *Religion under Socialism in China*. Trans. Donald E. MacInnis and Zheng Xi'an. Armonk, N.Y.: M. E. Sharpe. 1991.

Lyall, Leslie. *Come Wind, Come Weather: The Present Experience of the Church in China*. Chicago: Moody Press, 1960.

———. *A Passion for the Impossible: The China Inland Mission 1865–1965*. London: Hodder & Stoughton, 1965.

———. *Red Sky at Night: Communism Confronts Christianity in China*. London: Hodder & Stoughton, 1969.

———. *Three of China's Mighty Men*. London: Overseas Missionary Fellowship, 1973.

MacFarland, Charles S. *The New Church and the New Germany: A Study of Church and State*. New York: Macmillan, 1934.

MacInnis, Donald E. *Religion in China Today: Policy and Practice*. Maryknoll, N.Y.: Orbis, 1989.

———. *Religious Policy and Practice in Communist China: A Documentary History*. New York: MacMillan, 1972.

MacMillan, Ron. "Bishop Ting and China's House Churches." *Christian Century* 106 (August 16–23, 1989): 755–56.

Mao Zedong. *Mao Tse-tung and Lin Piao: Post Revolutionary Writings*. Edited by K. Fan. Garden City, N.Y.: Anchor, 1972.

———. *Selected Works of Mao Tse-tung*. 5 vols. Peking: Foreign Languages Press, 1965.

Marsden, George M. *Fundamentalism and American Culture: The Shaping of Twentieth-Century Evangelicalism 1870–1925*. Oxford: Oxford University Press, 1980.

Matheson, Peter. *The Third Reich and the Christian Churches: A Documentary Account of Christian Resistance and Complicity During the Nazi Era*. Edinburgh: T &T Clark, 1981.

Mead, George H. *Mind, Self, and Society*. Chicago: University of Chicago Press, 1934.

Milbank, John. *Theology and Social Theory: Beyond Secular Reason*. Oxford: Blackwell, 1990.

Milton, John. *John Milton: English Minor Poems, Paradise Lost, Samson Agonistes, Areopagitica*. Vol. 29 of *The Great Books of the Western World*. Chicago: Encyclopedia Britannica, 1992.

Murphy, David. "Mass Appeal." *Far Eastern Economic Review* Internet edition, 27 December 2001.

Ng Lee-ming. "Christianity and Social Change: The Case in China, 1920–1950." Diss., Princeton Theological Seminary, 1970.

———. "Wang Ming-Tao: An Evaluation of His Thought and Action." *Cheng Feng* 16 (1973): 51–80.

Niebuhr, H. Richard. *Christ and Culture*. New York: Harper & Row, 1951.

———. *The Meaning of Revelation*. New York: MacMillan, 1941.

———. *Radical Monotheism and Western Culture*. New York: Harper & Brothers, 1943.

———. *The Responsible Self*. New York: Harper & Row, 1963.

Orr, Robert G. *Religion in China*. New York: Friendship Press, 1980.

Packer, J. I. *Fundamentalism and the Word of God*. Grand Rapids: Eerdmans, 1958.

Paton, David M. *Christian Missions and the Judgement of God*. London: SCM, 1953.

Ramachandra, Vinoth. *Gods That Fail: Modern Idolatry and Christian Mission*. Carlisle: Paternoster, 1996.

Reynolds, Arthur, ed. *The Voice of China's Christians: Pathway to Glory*. London: OMF, 1973.

Scholder, Klaus. *The Churches and the Third Reich*. 2 vols. London: SCM, 1988.

Schwartz, Benjamin I. *In Search of Wealth and Power: Yen Fu and the West*. Cambridge: Harvard University Press, 1964.

Shea, Nina, "Atrocities Not Fit to Print." *First Things* 77 (November 1997): 32–35.

Smith, Anthony D. S. *Nationalism in the Twentieth Century*. New York: New York University Press, 1979.

Stassen, Glen H., D. M. Yeager, and John Howard Yoder. *Authentic Transformation: A New Vision of Christ and Culture*. Nashville: Abingdon, 1996.

Study Committee Report. "Shengjing Zhenli He Diguo Zhuyi Sixiang Juedui Bu Neng Tiaohe" ("Biblical Truth and Imperialist Poisonous Thought Are Absolutely Incompatible"). *Jin Ling Xie He Xue Yuan Zhi (Nanjing Theological Review)* 4 (November 1955): 29–37.

Szeto, Paul Cheuk-Ching. "Suffering in the Experience of the Protestant Church in China (1911–1980): A Chinese Perspective." Diss., Fuller Theological Seminary, 1980.

Tillich, Paul. *The Socialist Decision*. Translated by Franklin Sherman. London: Harper & Row, 1977.

Ting, K. H. "Zheng Gao Wang Ming Dao" ("A Stern Warning to Wang Mingdao"). *Tian Feng* 477–78 (August 8, 1955): 608–15.

Tow, Timothy. *John Sung My Teacher*. Singapore: Christian Life Publishers, 1985.

Van Slyke, Lyman P. *Enemies and Friends: The United-Front in Chinese Communist History*. Stanford, Calif.: Stanford University Press, 1967.

Varg, Paul A. *Missionaries, Chinese, and Diplomats: The American Protestant Movement in China, 1890–1952*. Princeton: Princeton University Press, 1958.

Wang, Mary. *The Chinese Church That Will Not Die*. London: Hodder & Stoughton, 1971.

Wang Mingdao. *A Call to the Church from Wang Ming-dao*. Edited by Leona F. Choy. Translated by Theodore Choy. Fort Washington Pa.: Christian Literature Crusade, 1983.

———. *Spiritual Food*. Translated by Arthur Reynolds. Southhampton, Eng.: Mayflower Christian Books, 1983.

———. *A Stone Made Smooth*. Southhampton, Eng.: Mayflower Christian Books, 1981.

———. *Wu Shi Nian Lai (After Fifty Years)*. Beijing: Spiritual Food Quarterly Special Publications, 1950.

———. *Wang Ming Dao Wen Ke (Treasuries of Wang Ming Dao)*. Edited by C. C. Wang. 7 vols. Taichung, Taiwan: Conservative Baptist Press, 1996.

Wang, Stephen C. H. *Wang Ming Dao: You Si Shi Nian (The Last Forty Years)*. Scarbourough, Ont.: Canada Gospel Publishing House. 1997.

Wang, Weifan. "Y. T. Wu and Wang Mingdao." *Chinese Theological Review* 5 (1989): 44–48.

Whincup, Greg. *The Heart of Chinese Poetry*. New York: Doubleday, 1987.

Whitehead, James D. "Christ, Salvation, and Maoism." In *China and Christianity: Historical and Future Encounters*, edited by James Whitehead, Yu-Ming Shaw, and N. J. Girardot, 231–52. Notre Dame, Ind.: University of Notre Dame Press, 1979.

Whyte, Bob. *Unfinished Encounter: China and Christianity*. Glasgow: Collins, 1988.

Wickeri, Philip Lauri. *Seeking the Common Ground: Protestant Christianity, the Three-Self Movement and China's United Front*. Maryknoll, N.Y.: Orbis, 1988.

Woo, Franklin J. "The Political Challenge of China to Western Christianity and Chinese Religion." *Missiology* 13 (July 1985): 347–52.

Yang, C. K. *Religion in Chinese Society: A Study of Contemporary Social Functions of Religion and Some of Their Historical Factors*. Berkeley and Los Angeles: University of California Press, 1961.

Yip, Ka-che. *Religion, Nationalism and Chinese Students: The Anti-Christian Movement of 1922–1927*. Bellingham, Wash.: Center for East Asian Studies, Western Washington University, 1980.

Yoder, John Howard. *The Priestly Kingdom: Social Ethics as Gospel*. Notre Dame, Ind.: University of Notre Dame Press, 1984.

———. *The Royal Priesthood: Essays Ecclesiological and Ecumenical*. Edited by Michael G. Cartwright. Grand Rapids: Eerdmans, 1994.

Young, Crawford. *The Politics of Cultural Pluralism*. Madison: University of Wisconsin Press, 1976.